setting

spirits

free

© Jim D'Angelo/D'Angelo Studio

About the Author

Diana Palm (Wisconsin) is a spiritual healer, certified Reiki master, and medium. She teaches classes throughout the United States on paranormal investigation, Theta Healing, and mediumship, and works with paranormal investigative groups to clear haunted locations. Theta Healing retreats are scheduled throughout the year in Menomonie, Wisconsin, and private sessions are available by phone. Visit Diana online at ConnectWithTheLight.com.

DIANA PALM

setting

spirits

free

Clear Negative Energy
& Help Ghosts Cross Over

Llewellyn Publications
Woodbury, Minnesota

FIRST EDITION
First Printing, 2013

Cover art: Window: iStockphoto.com/Evgeny Kuklev
            Sunset: iStockphoto.com/Peter Zelei
Cover design by Kevin R. Brown

Theta Healing is a registered trademark of Nature Path, Inc.

Llewellyn Publications is a registered trademark of Llewellyn Worldwide Ltd.

Library of Congress Cataloging-in-Publication Data
Palm, Diana.
  Setting spirits free : clear negative energy & help ghosts cross over / by Diana Palm. — First Edition.
      pages cm
  ISBN 978-0-7387-3573-3
  1. Ghosts. I. Title.
  BF1471.P35 2013
  133.1—dc23
                          2013007668

Llewellyn Publications
A Division of Llewellyn Worldwide Ltd.
2143 Wooddale Drive
Woodbury, MN 55125-2989
www.llewellyn.com

Printed in the United States of America

This book is dedicated to all people who seek the truth and answer the call to help the spirit world.

In loving memory of Dickie Cool Jr. and Mary Schlangen.

Contents

prologue

It was late one evening when I got the call. A friend of mine needed help. She had arrived home from work to find her house in disarray again. Her dog had been barking nonstop for three days and it was wearing on him. She was worried that her dog was not sleeping or eating because he was so distressed. I could hear him in the background: bark, growl, bark. It was nonstop, like she said. "I can't see who it is, but someone or something is here. Can you help me?"

I closed my eyes and went up to the light to connect. My friend lives in a different state, so I remotely viewed her house. Immediately, I felt the presence of several entities. Some were of the harmless, friendly type, and others were menacing and demonic. My friend explained to me that similar episodes had been happening in spurts and that the last time it happened she started wearing an amulet around her neck for protection. Then, she told me, her necklace had gone missing a few days earlier. One day it was in her jewelry box and the next day it was gone. She lived alone and knew that she had not misplaced the necklace. She felt strongly that the necklace protected her, so she was extra careful when taking it off to shower. When she went to retrieve it one day, it had literally disappeared. That was three days prior to her calling me and the onset of the hellish three days she had been living through.

I began to clear out the energies in and around her home while sending them back to God. The dog's reaction told me that he could see them leaving, but he did not feel safe enough to lie down or stop barking yet. I continued to remove wayward and attached spirits and then filled her home with light to neutralize the energy there. My friend gasped when she felt the shift. Everything went silent. Her dog felt it, too. He laid his exhausted little body down to rest, finally. The terror was over and the battle was won. The invisible intruders were gone, and he had done a good job protecting his family from what they could not see.

There was one more thing. I felt guided to a room at the end of the hallway. I had been to my friend's house only once before and knew that her bedroom was off to the left of the hallway, but I could not remember which room was to the right. I asked her to look down the hall and tell me if the door to the right was closed. "Yes," she confirmed. I asked her to go down the hall and open the door—something was in that room. Not knowing what this something could be, she was uneasy about the suggestion. But she looked down at her dog resting peacefully and felt her own sense of relief before she trustingly walked down the hall and opened that door.

Another gasp! It took a moment for her to tell me what it was that she had found. Lying on the floor just inside the room was her necklace that had mysteriously disappeared! She explained that she never went in that room. It was a spare room and there was no way that her necklace could have ended up in there. She fumbled with the phone a minute while I stayed connected with her energy to see this through. A moment later, I saw a beautiful blue energy emanate from all around her, and I both felt and saw the Virgin Mary. I told her that the Virgin Mary had just arrived and that she was all around her. Then my friend told me that she had just put her necklace back on and that it was the Miraculous Medal of the Virgin Mary.

I wasn't always able to hone my abilities as effectively as just described. As you continue reading this book, I will share with you what has worked for me and how you, too, can confidently work with the spirit world.

introduction

There are many great books available about spirituality and dozens about ghost busting, or what we now call paranormal investigating. However, there seems to be a void in educating the ghost enthusiast about the spirit world and how to discern spirits. Attempting to communicate with a ghost can be fun and exciting until you encounter something menacing or potentially harmful.

Thankfully, there are many paranormal investigation groups that are equipped to come to your home and help you. Although some groups will be able to identify the ghost and capture compelling evidence, they may not know how to get rid of the unwanted visitor for you. Most of the training offered from within paranormal groups comes in the form of how to use devices and review evidence. There isn't much offered in the way of understanding etheric beings or how to clear a home of an angry ghost. The purpose of this book is to show you how you can communicate safely and effectively with the spirit world and how to get rid of a haunting.

I am a Theta Healing instructor and teach people how to communicate with spirits. My main focus is healing, which includes working with spirits who have not crossed over into the light. Many of my clients come to see me when they are struggling through grief over the loss of a loved one. During a healing session, their loved one often appears to me. I can tell if the spirit needs help crossing over or if they are just popping in to offer love and support. I have been able to use my abilities to clear haunted houses and have worked with several paranormal investigation groups. Over the years, many paranormal groups from around the world have contacted me to assist them with difficult cases. My abilities enable me to send away darker entities that many groups avoid working with. I have had opportunities to clear houses remotely, communicate with patients in a coma, energetically close down portals, and send demonic entities away for good. My abilities to work with the spirit world have enhanced my work as a paranormal investigator, medium, and healer.

Anyone can do the work I do. It may take a little time to learn the nuances of working with the spirit world, but this book will show you how to use the theta brain wave to achieve communication with the other side. With expanded awareness of how the spirit world operates, you will be able to clear a haunted house and be open to communicate with a loved one who has passed. Spiritual education will increase your understanding of and efficacy in working with both ghosts and spirits. The information in this book has been gathered over a lifetime of working with spirits directly. As your knowledge of the spirit world grows, you will feel more confident in sending away dark entities and maintaining a clear home.

Someone who communicates with the spirit world is referred to as a medium. A medium has the distinct advantage of knowing when a spirit is present and can use their own body and mind to communicate. Everyone has the potential to become a medium. I believe that we are all born open to these abilities and that we slowly close them down as we grow older. Some mediums keep their abilities from early childhood, and others develop their skills as an adult. We will learn why we close down our abilities and learn how to reopen ourselves to the spirit world around us.

While most mediums can access the spirit world more readily than the general public can, it does not mean that they are necessarily adept at helping ghosts. In order to clear a ghost or haunted house, the medium will need to have a deeper understanding of the inner workings of the spirit world. Most mediums can establish a connection with a person's deceased loved one, but they may not know the difference between a ghost that is trapped and a spirit that has crossed over into the light, and they may not know how to cross over a trapped soul. This book will explain the types of spirit energy that you may encounter and how to help each one.

The other issue we encounter while working with the spirit world is the darker entities that wreak havoc on the living. We will discuss how those spirits present themselves and how you can easily and safely send them away. Trust me, if you spend some time in the theta brain wave, you *will* see all kinds of spirits. They exist in different frequencies and tend to hang around the living without being detected. Soon you will be able to see into other spiritual dimensions that may have been invisible to you before. It is important to note that with the techniques in this book, you can send away any type of entity.

In this book I will refer to my connection to the light, and sometimes I will say "God" or "Creator." I am not speaking from any one religious perspective. When I say that I am connecting with the Creator, I am really addressing the Creator of All That Is, or God. I am not referring to someone that any one particular religion has claimed as its own. It doesn't matter what religion you follow, if any. Everyone has the divine right to connect to the light and access the Creator of All That Is.

To achieve spirit communication, discern spirits, and be able to cross over ghosts, we will be using the theta brain wave to access higher dimensions in the light that will connect us to the Creator energy. If you are completely new to this concept, don't worry—I will show you how to get there. For those of you who currently work with the light, this may be a higher connection in the light than you have used in the past. When you tap into this energy, you will not get drained, get caught up in drama, or be limited to what you can see. Spirit communication will become easy and your messages will be clear. To explain why the Theta Healing technique is so effective, you will need a basic understanding of brain waves. This will be explained in chapter 2, "The Light."

Many people seek to understand and communicate with the spirit world for a variety of reasons. Some of you may have lost a loved one with whom you wish to reestablish contact. Some of you may be living in a haunted house, and some of you may be working with a paranormal team and want to beef up your abilities. A vibrational shift has happened on our planet, and many people are experiencing paranormal events and seeing ghosts for the first time. It is important to understand that these beings were always here and existed around us but were invisible to the human eye. Now that more people are able to see them, reported hauntings have increased dramatically and people are desperately seeking help. I assure you, you are not losing your mind. Take a deep breath ... and continue reading to learn how you can clear the spiritual dimensions around you and keep your home safe.

1: eyes wide open

I have been working with the spirit world for most of my life. From as early as I can remember, the spirit world has held a fascination for me that is unequaled. When I was young, I remember traveling to ghost towns and feeling overwhelmed with sadness for all the lost souls. I didn't always see ghosts, but I could feel them around me. As I grew into adolescence, my experiences became more auditory and visual.

I was raised in an Orthodox Catholic family and feared that something was wrong with me because of my experiences with spirits. One time I told my mother about a spirit that came to see me after I had been praying for divine guidance, and she said that it was probably the Devil in disguise. I knew that the spirit was a messenger of light, because after the visit I experienced absolute clarity about a difficult situation I was going through. However, my mother's words stayed with me, as often happens when our parents offer guidance of any kind. Though I didn't doubt what I had seen that night, her advice urged me to learn how to discern spirits.

My mother's devotion to God had her spending most of her time in prayer, and she would sometimes share that she had visions or visits from angels. The words *psychic* and *medium* were not used in our house, and any comments about them were mostly negative. I grew up feeling that I definitely did not want to accept that part of me unless I was sure it was good. Needless to say, I spent countless hours in the library researching the subject from a purely scientific point of view. Then, in 1995, I traveled as a spiritual pilgrim to Medjugorje, where I encountered a holy priest who had psychic abilities. If a person purposely left out some of their sins during confession, he would remind them of what they were. I finally accepted the belief that intuitive gifts were not bad at all, but should be used for the good of humanity.

There were several very dark periods in my life when I felt completely alone and unsupported. Each time, a voice would call out to me in a clear and audible fashion, and though I didn't know who it was, it seemed familiar to me. Hearing this voice changed things for me, because I realized that I was never really alone. I accepted this voice as a call from my guardian angel and knew that I was being protected by the spirit world.

Before I decided to get pregnant, my future daughter called to me from the spirit world, too. That really put me in a pinch, because at the time I was going through a divorce and didn't have a partner. She told me that she would be a girl and that her name was Alanna. When I looked up the name, I discovered it meant "awakening." Yes, I intuitively knew that she would be my awakening, because I would have to learn many things in order to be a good mother to her. I could feel her precious little soul waiting for me to conceive, and I knew that she hung around me in spirit before she was born.

During my pregnancy, I was hospitalized for six weeks on bed rest. I cherished the time I had to connect with my baby by reading spiritual books and poetry to her while rubbing my big belly. My amniotic fluid was dangerously low, so the doctors followed our progress closely from day to day. I kept a journal during my hospital stay and found it interesting that when I wanted to go home, my amniotic fluid would increase, and when I wanted to stay in the hospital, it would decrease. Home for me at that time was not a stable place to be, so I preferred the care I received at the hospital. When I finally gave birth via C-section, the team of doctors studied our case. They could find no physical reason for my condition or why it had fluctuated depending on my needs, and we remained a medical mystery.

We lived in the desert out West in one of my grandparents' cottages when I began to see nightly visitors in my room. I didn't know who they were, why they were there, or how to protect my baby from them. A woman I met told me that I could send away anything by saying, "I am protected in the light of Christ." Each time an apparition appeared in my room, I would wrap my arms around my baby and repeat those words until I fell asleep. We moved shortly after that, but the experiences continued. I was on the brink of learning all about the spirit world from the vantage point of experience.

I could see how connected Alanna was to the spirit world, and other people commented on it, too. When we went shopping, women in the store would rush over to rub the top of her head and ask to hold her. She was like a bright light that everyone wanted to touch. Sometimes she would stare intently at the space in front of her and respond as if she were being talked to. She would suddenly giggle as if an invisible grandmother were poking her belly. I could sense spirit energy around my daughter, but I could not see it, so I prayed over her every night. I would recite this prayer:

Angel of God, my guardian dear,
to whom his love commits me here.
Ever this day, be at my side,
to light, to guard, to rule, to guide.
Amen.

We were visiting my mother one evening when my daughter was just eighteen months old. She was an early talker, and I documented all the words and phrases she could say in her baby book. There were many, but mostly only one- and two-word combinations. So it was more than uncanny when she managed to recite an entire prayer one night. Grandma was going to bed, and I said to my daughter, "What do we say at bedtime?" Thinking that she might close her eyes and bow her head, she surprised me when she folded her delicate little fingers and said the entire prayer, word for word, in her baby vernacular. It was impossible for me to wrap my mind around, and my mother and I both gasped in surprise. *How did she do that?* A shiver went through my body, and I was both thrilled and freaked out at the same time. I knew the angels were around my daughter, but it wasn't until she was three years old that she told me about the others she could see.

We were living in the Midwest, where I had spent most of my life growing up. I raised my daughter alone, and we lived in many historic homes in my hometown. Alanna sometimes knew things before they happened and would tell me when someone was coming to visit. I would assure her that the person she mentioned lived hours away and was not coming over. But she would draw a picture for them anyway and hand it to me with their name on it. Time and time again, she was right. We would get an unexpected visit from one of our friends or relatives from out of town.

We were aware of the spiritual presence around us and accepted the strange things that occurred in all the places we lived. It was common for us to hear voices chatting at night and to hear music that wasn't being played. Antique doorknobs would twist and turn, and doors would open by themselves. Light bulbs would explode, and we could hear footsteps walk across wooden floors in rooms that were empty. Things seemed to move from one location to another on their own. Alanna spent countless hours playing in her room, drawing and sometimes talking to our invisible guests that followed us each time we moved. She would often tell me about the man who would wake her up at night and stand at the foot of her bed. At one point she said, "Mama, next time we move, can we please live in a house that isn't haunted?" I explained that I didn't think that would be possible, because she just saw things.

I observed that my daughter was more open to the spirit world than I was and that she could see more than I could. I longed to be as open as she was so I could see what she was seeing. That desire marked the beginning of my journey to learn all I could about the spirit world. As her mother, it was my job to protect her connection and to support her natural state of openness. I didn't want religious dogma or thoughtless grownups to make her doubt herself. When she encountered ghosts, I would very calmly ask her if they needed our help. Alanna was able to tell me details about what she saw and what they wanted.

When my daughter was four years old, she told her babysitter that she would heal her pain with her magic hands. That afternoon, the babysitter called me frantically, exclaiming that we needed to have her tested at the university right away. "She healed me!" The babysitter had suffered from grand mal seizures, and one of the after-effects was a debilitating headache that lasted for days. But when my daughter offered to heal her, the pain went away within minutes. I told the sitter that I was coming right over to pick her up and that she should not call anyone about this. I explained that it was completely normal and natural for us to be able to heal each other and that I did not want my daughter turned into some kind of lab rat by people who didn't understand that. A healing priest once told me that we were all supposed to heal each other because there weren't enough of them to go around. Why was something so natural received with such disbelief?

By the time my daughter was in second grade, we had learned to keep our experiences quiet. She could still see spirits, but her friends at school could not. While she was playing joyfully with her spirit friends and angel guardians, the other kids didn't understand. Sometimes she would come home from school concerned that her friends couldn't see all the wonderful angels around them that were trying to help them. She would get upset that so many of her school friends were oblivious to the angels, and she didn't understand why some of them did mean things to each other. Many of those children had already been yanked away from their spiritual connection and had been told that things didn't exist if they could not be seen. I didn't want my daughter to lose her connection as well, so we agreed to share our experiences only with each other in the safety of our home. It was kind of like having our own little secret world, and we knew that we were free to completely be ourselves when we were together. No subject was off-limits, and that allowed our imagination and spiritual expansion fertile ground.

I was in my thirties the first time I encountered a deceased loved one in spirit. I had been dating an older gentleman who had been widowed. Our relationship was new, and our dating habits were pretty self-serving at the time. He would often sleep over at my house and then sneak home in the early morning for his teenage daughter, who was there alone. One early morning, he slipped out of bed to go home, and I encountered his late wife standing in the doorway of my bedroom. She was beautiful and full of light. She had flowing brown hair and wore a long white nightgown. I knew immediately who it was even though I hadn't seen a picture of her. I don't remember any actual words that she spoke, but I knew that in some way she was passing the parental torch to me. After her visit, we restructured our relationship and always included his daughter in our plans. We did a lot more family-oriented things that involved all our kids.

Seeing the apparition of a loved one made sense to me because the desire to look after loved ones does not end with physical death. Visitations such as these are readily accepted and anticipated by most people of a variety of faiths. However, this was the first time I recall witnessing the apparition of a loved one in spirit. Then one night, I awoke and saw a man pass by my bedroom doorway. His appearance was not filled with light like the other apparition. It didn't seem divine like the being of light I had experienced, either. I assumed it was a real man walking down the dark hallway. Alanna was sleeping beside me, so I gently slipped out of bed and went to confront the intruder. As a single mother, I knew that I must protect my daughter even if I was terrified. When I turned the corner, the man vanished. I searched the entire apartment, and all the doors and windows were locked. When I finally settled back into bed, I realized that I had witnessed a full-bodied apparition of a ghost! Each night, this ghost would appear and walk past my bedroom doorway before he disappeared. When I needed to use the bathroom, I would sit in the dark and wait for him to pass by before running down the hall. He didn't attempt to communicate, but he appeared nightly like clockwork.

Most of our friends didn't know what we were experiencing until I felt prompted to call in a paranormal investigation group for validation. They collected many EVPs (electronic voice phenomena, or spirit voices on a tape recording) and photographed many strange anomalies. The story of our haunted house ran on the front page of the *St. Paul Pioneer Press* and was included in a book of area hauntings.

After the investigation, the paranormal activity in the house seemed to increase. We had always coexisted with the ghosts in a peaceful way, but the increased activity made me think they needed our help desperately. I began to research the property and discovered that our house was built upon a potter's field, or an old cemetery, from the 1800s. The microfilm was stored at the library, and a historian helped me to navigate through newspaper articles until we found what we were looking for. The article claimed that the townspeople had been in an uproar when the developers began to build upon the land without moving the bodies buried there. Some of our neighbors had even found a headstone while digging in their yard to put in a pool.

We decided to invite the paranormal group back to help us cross over the ghosts that were trapped there. During their send-off, we captured EVPs in different voices that said, "I love you," "We love you," and "Alanna." It was a bit unsettling for me to hear my daughter's name being called to from the spirit world, but I knew they were familiar with us and had spent a lot of time trying to communicate with her.

I perceived my experiences with the spirit world as something that just happened to me and not something that I did. I didn't know that I could learn to work with the spirit world in any kind of purposeful way. All of that changed for me when I lost my best friend. His death devastated me so deeply that the only inspiration I had to keep living came from the signs he sent me from the other side. One night, he sent me a powerful dream visit. We were boating on the river and the wind was blowing through my hair. I was elated to spend time with him again. Then he offered to take me with him. I realized that I had a choice to stay on earth or go with him into the spirit world. Immediately, my thoughts turned to my daughter, and I told him that I was going to stay. Alanna had been my choice since the moment I decided to have her, and she was my choice still. Just as those words left my mouth, a powerful gust of wind blew through my hair again, but this time it altered the scene of my dream. I was sitting on the shore of the river with my daughter on my lap. She was young again, and the water lapped gently over us as I told her about my encounter. She said, "Oh, Mama. You should have gone with him. You would have had so much more fun with him." To which I replied, "You have always been my choice.

But at least I got to feel the wind in my hair." I awoke in tears as I realized this to be true. His spirit was like the wind that blew life into the stillness. His vitality and love of life were contagious to everyone who knew him, and I often felt more alive with him than I had ever felt before.

I came to understand that my best friend had not left my side when he passed because he was so good at leaving me signs of his presence. He continued to meet me in dreams, was able to move things, and once appeared in a photo. My longing to keep my connection to him motivated me to learn more about communicating with the other side. I knew that in order to heal, I must develop my abilities and those parts of myself that I feared.

Communicating with a deceased loved one was something I hadn't done before, but I knew it was time for me to finally learn how. I began to take classes and work on my spiritual development when I had time. But when my little sister died a few years later, it prompted me to completely change the direction of my life. Although my business was successful, I was too busy to find time for my spiritual work. That had made me feel imbalanced, and I longed for more connection. My sister's death sent me into hours of quiet meditation and prayer, and I knew that it was time to change everything in my life. It was almost as if her spirit were urging me do what I loved and came here to do.

The first mediumship class I took put all my fears to rest. My teacher and mentor was very wise, and his approach was to be of service, not to feed the ego. He passed away about a year after I met him and seemed to continue his teaching from the other side. After that, I bounced around from circle to circle and from class to class in order to continue my spiritual development, but I was unable to find a good fit. I once confided in a teacher that I wanted to "see" spirits better, and she replied, "No one sees spirits, because they are just energy. It's not like the TV show *Ghost Whisperer.*" I didn't understand why she seemed so condescending toward me. The plain truth was that I *had* seen spirits. I had seen both those that had crossed and those that were trapped on the earthly plane. A teacher who admittedly had never seen a spirit would not have much to teach me, so I kept looking.

Then everything changed for me. I found a healing modality called Theta Healing, and it delivered everything that it promised. Suddenly, I was able to do things that I always hoped I would be able to do. In the very first class, I was able to see visions in my mind's eye and know what types of spirits were in the room. When I was feeling "blocked," I could find out the reason and then clear the block in an instant. Through this technique, I was able to clear many of my beliefs and fears surrounding the spirit world, which allowed me to access it with clarity.

My spiritual vision became clearer as I continued to do healing work with clients. Sometimes I would get a feeling that my client was bringing a deceased loved one with them before they would show up for the session. If I took a moment, I would know who it was ahead of time. But other times I encountered them intuitively during the healing session. I could see that the spirits who accompanied my clients received part of the healing as well.

I always tell my clients when a loved one in spirit shows up during a healing session. Oftentimes my clients ask for their departed family member or friend to be with them when they come to work with me. When I mention that a particular loved one is present with them and it is the person they asked for, it serves as validation for my client. However, I wanted to improve my ability to identify spirits through evidence. Every now and then, my ego would kick in and try to prevent me from advancing. It would say things to me like, "Who do you think you are? You can't really talk to spirits." I recognized this as fear. Fear of failure. And like most things that I have ever feared in my life, I decided to tackle it for that very reason.

After clearing my fear-based beliefs by using the Theta Healing technique, I sought out a reputable medium to work with. His spiritual development circles didn't fit my schedule, but he was willing to work with me one on one. The very first time we met, he put me in the hot seat and told me to do a mediumship reading for him. That was exactly what I needed. He watched me as I went up to connect to the light through the theta brain wave and then allowed me to give him a message from spirit. Most of my information was coming in the form of feeling or sensing, so he offered a visualization technique to help clear up my vision. He said that once I had established contact with a spirit, I should be of service to them. He suggested that I pretend to go shopping with the spirit to see what they liked to wear. Once I knew what type of clothes they liked, I would be able to see them clearly, without the pressure of trying to see them right away. He asked me to connect to another ancestor of his and to approach the reading from a service standpoint. The technique worked really well, and I brought through an ancestor of his with such clarity that even he was surprised. When our session was over, he told me to go home and do another reading for someone using the technique he had shown me.

I went straight home and sat down in my healing room to work on my mediumship skills. The moment I sat down, I realized that I didn't have anyone to work with. The first person who popped into my mind was a close friend I had known for most of my life. I knew she was busy working, but I decided to connect to an ancestor of hers and write down any information I got. She could validate the information later, I thought. I went up to the light and connected with one of her ancestors. Immediately an older man appeared. Her ancestor showed scenes of himself as a much younger man, probably from an age when he was most proud of himself. He was wearing a bomber jacket and was quite handsome. He continued to show me scenes from his lifetime and impressed upon me that he felt he had let his daughter down. I intuitively knew this man was my friend's grandfather. He felt like he had failed his own daughter and that he hadn't been there for her. He blamed himself for the reason she struggled so much in life. When he was done explaining all this to me, he got quieter, like he wanted to make sure I was paying attention. Then he said,

"When the time is right, I will be there for her." He really wanted to make sure that she knew he would be there for her.

I gave the entire message to my friend, who was able to validate most of the information, right down to the way he dressed. The following day, she called her mother for clarification of the things she didn't know. She read the entire message to her mother. Thankfully, her mother was able to validate everything else.

My friend's mother had been quite ill for years, and although everyone knew she was sick, no one expected her to die anytime soon. However, the day after this message from spirit was shared with her, she passed peacefully at home. When my friend called frantically to tell me about her mother passing, all she could say was that she had died alone. She felt terrible because she hadn't been with her.

Through her tears, I could hear her pain. A moment of silence filled the car and all around me as this news of her death settled in. Her mother had been a special person in my life. She had often taken me in and let me stay with them when I didn't have anywhere else to go. *Ring, ring.* The phone began to ring again. A sigh of relief came over me. It was my friend again—however, this time her voice sounded peaceful. "She didn't die alone. My grandfather was with her. Thank you for the message you gave us. It is the only thing that gives me peace right now." Silence ....I realized right then and there how mysterious and magical the spirit world was and how very special it had been for me to be able to be a part of this message and healing.

At last, I was able to work with the spirit world in a meaningful way. I learned how to connect to a spirit and how to get a message. My spiritual eyes were wide open. I believe that this ability is within all of us. Perhaps it has been dormant in you up until now, or perhaps you have begun to experience things that you cannot explain. In the next chapter, I will give you the technique that will allow you to access the spirit world with confidence and purpose.

2: the light

So you want to see ghosts and communicate with the spirit world, but you don't know where to start? If you're like a lot of people out there, you have already tried meditating with a certain degree of success, read many books, followed the work of famous mediums, and taken spiritual development classes. At least, that's who I imagine I'm talking to at this point. If you haven't done any of those things yet but find yourself in the same place waiting for the next initiation or big leap forward, then perhaps I can save you some time!

While it's no secret that I did all those things myself, they are not what got me to where I am today. I'm about to share something with you that may change the way you have developed your abilities up until this point. The tool I'm going to share with you is immediate and accessible for everyone. Theta Healing and the use of the theta brain wave helped me to connect instantly and purposefully to the spirit world. Although Theta Healing is centered on clearing beliefs, you won't need to take a class or become a practitioner to use the techniques described in this book. I will show you how to achieve the theta brain wave on your own. However, if you wish to take a class or become a Theta Healing practitioner, classes are available worldwide.

Before we go any further, it is important to explain the brain waves and why using the theta brain wave is so powerful. I will also include my "Road Map to the Light" technique, which will help you to achieve the theta brain wave.

There are basically five frequencies of brain waves:

- **Beta**—Any time you are thinking, talking, or doing, your mind is in the beta brain wave. Right now, you are most likely in beta, with a brain wave frequency of 14–28 cycles per second. Most of us spend the majority of our day being active and alert in beta.

- **Alpha**—Many people who meditate or do healing work will be familiar with the alpha brain wave. The alpha brain wave is slower than beta, with a frequency of 7–14 cycles per second. When you experience relaxation, daydreams, or some forms of healing (such as Reiki), you are in the alpha brain wave.

- **Theta**—The theta brain wave is even slower than alpha and is noted by a very deep state of relaxation. The theta brain wave is often achieved during hypnosis or dreaming while asleep, and the frequency is only 4–7 cycles per second. It used to be only sages, Tibetan monks, and shamans who knew how to access this sleeping brain wave through hours of meditation and fasting. There are many benefits to using this brain wave, which I will discuss in detail.

- **Delta**—When you are in a deep sleep, you are in the delta brain wave. The delta brain wave slows to a frequency of 0–4 cycles per second.

- **Gamma**—Gamma is the brain wave of higher learning, mental activity, and a hyper-alert state in which to process information. The gamma brain wave frequency can be 40+ cycles per second.

While we use all of the brain waves in any given day, we can actually train ourselves to use certain ones more than others. We can literally recode our subconscious mind with the use of the theta brain wave, because that is where our subconscious programs are stored. The theta brain wave has long been associated with higher levels of consciousness, connection to higher dimensions, and inner vision. The shamanic state of consciousness is achieved in the theta brain wave, allowing you to journey into higher planes and realities. It is possible to induce a theta brain wave through steady, rhythmic drumming at the same rate as the waves themselves. Tibetan Buddhist chants transport the monks into realms of higher consciousness as they follow this rhythm. Theta meditation spurs creativity, reduces stress, awakens intuition, and opens the door to what many people consider to be "supernatural" abilities. Mystics often use the theta brain wave to heal instantly. Accessing this brain wave allows you to tap into guidance directly from the source.

Vianna Stibal, creator of the Theta Healing technique, learned that it was possible to access the theta brain wave in a moment and that you could literally train your brain to do it on command. She has proven the efficacy of the technique through use of electroencephalography, or EEG (which measures brain waves). In 2006, I stumbled into a Theta Healing class, and it enhanced all my abilities instantly. While I had spent many hours attempting to meditate, I had seldom reached the state of euphoria associated with that practice. It seemed like I had wasted a lot of time trying to achieve what I now was able to do in a moment. I didn't have to disregard any of the other things I learned, because they could all still be used in the altered theta state.

When I began to use this brain wave, I was suddenly able to move mountains instead of feeling that I was constantly climbing them. The Theta Healing technique allowed me to go into my subconscious mind and change the fear-based programs that held me back. I was able to reprogram my belief system to match my conscious beliefs so that issues of struggle were diminished. The more I used Theta Healing to clear myself, the more light and truth could reach me. It is simply the fastest way to heal and develop spiritually that I have ever experienced.

The path to experiencing the waking theta brain wave is simple. Most people can reach this state very quickly and find their way back to it simply by intending. Some people may have a little trouble reaching the theta brain wave, but with a little persistence, it will happen. Most young children spend a lot of time in the theta brain wave, which explains why so many children have the natural ability to see spirits. When you spend any amount of time in the theta brain wave, you will feel divinely connected to everything in creation. You may feel euphoric and energized at the same time, and you will have greater mental clarity than you have ever experienced before. It is a spiritual feeling of knowing that you are one with all that is, without separation. It is from within this brain wave that I achieve my communication with the spirit world.

There is a simple road map to follow that will help you achieve the theta brain wave to access the light. The road map requires that you send your consciousness above your space through your crown chakra. The act of going above your space to connect with the light will put you in the alpha brain wave. It has been proven that when you go there and say the word "God" (or "Creator"), your brain actually shifts into the theta brain wave. It doesn't matter what your beliefs are in terms of religion or spirituality. This process works for anyone having a faith in some sort of higher power. Calling upon whichever higher power you believe in will shift your brain into the theta brain wave.

When you begin to use the theta brain wave, you will be able to experience things that you may not have experienced before. Knowing that you are able to connect to the spirit world may shift your paradigm dramatically. Yes, you can become a medium. You can work with the angels and visit with your loved ones on the other side. You don't have to be born from a band of gypsies or raised in remote mountains to harness the gifts that a slower brain wave offers. Scientists are beginning to understand the things that were once considered unexplainable as they dispel the centuries-old misunderstandings about the spirit world. Ordinary people have access to higher dimensions if they are willing to develop the skills. There are different methods to connect to the light, to train your brain, and to focus with your spiritual sight, but I'm going to teach you the one that works for me.

"Road Map to the Light" Technique

Begin by sitting comfortably in a place where you will not be disturbed. Close your eyes. Slowly breathe in, filling your lungs to capacity, and then breathe out through pursed lips. Taking a few deep breaths will help to center and ground you. Imagine that you are connected with Mother Earth and that you are anchored to the physical world. Now imagine that a beautiful energy coming up from inside the earth is moving into you. Starting with your feet, you will feel this energy move through your body, igniting and opening all of your chakras on the way up. This process allows you to check your chakras, because if any are closed, it will be difficult for you to connect to the light properly.

Visualize that as the energy reaches each of the chakras, they are spinning and open and balanced. It is wise to ask that your chakras are all functioning in your highest and best way so you don't unwittingly make changes that would throw off your energetic system. Asking that all things be done in the highest and best way removes our ego and allows the Creator to give us something that may be much better than what we are asking for.

Once you get used to this process, you will be able to access the theta brain wave in a second. But while you are learning and training yourself where to go, take your time. The process will speed up on its own through repetition. Imagine that each chakra is spinning clockwise, starting with your root chakra (base of spine), then your sacral chakra (just below the navel), solar plexus chakra (above the navel in the stomach area), heart chakra (breastbone or chest), throat chakra (hollow of the throat), third eye chakra (middle of forehead), and crown chakra (top of head). You can even place your hand directly over each chakra and feel it open in the palm of your hand like a flower. When you are certain that all your chakras are open and functioning properly, you may continue.

Imagine that you are sending your consciousness out through your crown chakra on top of your head. Go above your space … until you visualize light. If you have done something similar before through another type of training, it is likely that you have been to this light before. However, keep going …. There is more light ahead. Continue to imagine that you are going further out into space and that you pass through many more lights. Keep going until you reach a pure, iridescent white light. When you enter this light, you may feel your eyelids start to flutter gently. If they aren't, you will need to go higher still.

The gentle fluttering of the eyelids signifies that you have entered the theta brain wave. When you dream, you experience REM (rapid eye movement) and are in the theta brain wave. When you hold a waking theta brain wave, your eyes will gently flutter as well, and you will visualize pure white light.

It may take some practice to hold a theta brain wave for any length of time, but with practice, it will be instant and you will be able to hold it for as long as you want. Once you have trained yourself to connect there, your brain will remember it and bring you there faster.

This is the energy of creation, or what some people call God or the Creator. It is here that you will go to connect to the light, and here where you will set clear intentions about what you want. The Theta Healing technique does this through a command process that signals your brain that this will happen. It is here that we stop asking for something to happen or hope that something will happen. When we are connected to the energy of creation, we operate at our highest potential as a co-creator. To see spirits, you will command (silently and while still connected):

Creator, it is commanded to see and communicate with _____ (deceased loved one's name) now. Thank you.

You may use whatever wording you choose to identify the highest energy in creation. Please do not use guides in this process, because the intention is to connect higher with the highest light. Recognize that this light exists in you— which allows you to access it. The command process simply tells your own brain that THIS WILL HAPPEN and removes the blocks that the ego uses to keep us feeling limited or full of doubt.

Next, imagine dropping down from the iridescent white light and, with your eyes still closed, focus on the energy in front of you. You may experience this spirit as a hologram or a soul light—either is okay. Your energy is still connected up above to the Creator, but you must go to a lower plane where the spirit world exists. God, or the Creator, is the highest energy in creation, and connecting to the energy there will allow you to use the theta brain wave instantly. You may even speak with your angels, guides, or other ascended masters simply by making the command. A command is a clear intention while being connected to the Creator's energy.

Spend some time there and get used to using the theta brain wave. The more you go there, the easier it will be to access this state in the future. You won't need to spend hours meditating to get there, either. Once your brain knows where you want to go, it will be simple.

We will be using the theta brain wave to connect to the light throughout this book. We will use this connection to communicate with spirits and ghosts. We will also use this connection to cross over ghosts and send entities away.

In my many years of experience, I have found that the most effective way to work with the spirit world is by using the theta brain wave and simple commands. Always show gratitude to God and the spirit world if you want them to continue working with you. Gratitude helps to open your heart's receptiveness to spirit communication.

3: what are ghosts?

The spirit world is a normal part of the physical world we live in. We are constantly surrounded by spiritual beings regardless of whether we can see them or not. Sightings of ghosts have been reported since the beginning of time. So what are they and why are they here? Why do only certain people see them? What do they want? In this chapter we will learn how a person becomes a ghost and what that means in the spirit world.

In order to become a ghost, a choice must be made. When a person dies, they leave the body that once housed their spirit and are no longer confined to a physical existence. Most spirits hang around to attend their own funeral. During this period, the spirit often visits family and friends, which is why so many people report seeing their deceased loved ones. The spirit maintains their connection to the Creator through what is called the "god cord." They may use that connection to cross over or go into the light at any time. The god cord is visible to an intuitive person and looks like a beam of light that emanates from the crown chakra up to God. In ancient art, it was depicted by a halo of light surrounding a holy person.

Every living person has a god cord. Depending on a person's state of healing, the light can be bright or dim, but we all have one. The god cord keeps the spirit connected to the heavens so that they can easily transition into the spirit world. They are usually met by loved ones who have passed before them and are escorted into the light, where they will patiently wait for all of their loved ones to eventually join them.

Life continues on the other side, and a spirit can make additional spiritual progress by what they learn and heal. Sometimes a spirit will choose to spend time with a living person that they feel compelled to help from the afterlife. This is healing for both the spirit and the living person and is not a haunting. As the spirit continues to grow in light on the other side, their frequency increases and they ascend into higher levels within the light. This is the normal path that a spirit takes after death. However, not all spirits go into the light right away.

Immediately following death, a spirit still has free will. The spirit can choose to follow their god cord up to the light at any time during the nine days following death. After the ninth day, the window of opportunity to cross over is temporarily lost. Somehow our ability to cross over into a higher vibrational frequency (the spirit world) can be limited to openings in the earth's natural energetic grid system. It is similar to the window in space time that NASA observes when planning the launch of space shuttles. Our spirit has a similar window of opportunity when it is easiest to cross from the physical plane into the spirit world. From all my experiences working with spirits, I have determined that the only way to get stuck here is by choice.

Some spirits turn away from the light because they are afraid that God will punish them for something. Others choose to stay behind because they have small children to look after, and other spirits stay because they have unfinished issues to heal with the living. While some spirits are afraid of the light, others are roaming around still confused and don't even know that they are dead.

So what happens to the spirits that turn away from the light? If a spirit stays behind out of free will for any reason, they surrender their ability to move on in the spirit world. Essentially, they are stuck between earth and the spirit world and exist at a frequency between the two. The frequency is slightly higher than earth and lower than the spirit world. We refer to these low-frequency spirits as ghosts. A ghost has limited ability to travel and usually attaches to a person, place, or thing. They tend to feel the way they did at the time of their death. If a person died in a drug-induced haze, then that is how they will appear as a ghost. If they died on a battlefield and suffered tremendous pain, they still feel that pain. The only relief that can be provided for a ghost is to cross it over and send it into the light to be healed.

Many people aren't aware that after a ghost is crossed over, it can come back and visit loved ones as a spirit. Some people hold the romantic notion that they will stay behind as a ghost to remain with their loved ones after death. While that may seem like a loving gesture, it is not quite accurate. Let me save you hundreds of years of roaming around in the dark to tell you how this works. When a "ghost" is crossed over into the light, it raises its vibration and becomes a "spirit." A spirit can be with all their loved ones simultaneously and is not trapped in one location. A spirit can appear to loved ones and help them from the other side. They are not in pain and, in fact, are filled with a peace and love that can come only from merging with the light. A ghost, on the other hand, is mostly caught up in their drama because they haven't been healed yet of earthly issues and pain. They no longer have free will and are limited by where they can go and what they can do. They must drain energy from the living in order to sustain themselves, and they remain unhealed.

Long-term exposure to ghost energy can make a person sick and depressed. It can also keep the family and loved ones from moving on from grief. So please don't think you're doing your loved ones any favors by hanging out on this plane past your expiration date. Go into the light where you will really be able to help them!

The Catholic religion refers to a place called "purgatory," where souls go when they are not allowed to enter heaven. I spent countless hours as a child praying for the lost souls that were trapped there. Purgatory is the closest thing to explain where these ghosts exist, with the main difference being that it was a personal choice and not a punishment. The vibration varies with ghosts that are trapped, and they can exhibit anything from confusion and dissatisfaction to pure anger.

How long does a ghost stay in limbo living between the earth and the spirit world? Eventually, the window of opportunity will open again and allow the ghost to cross over. However, this opening could be in fifty years or even three hundred years into the future. It could be any amount of time. The ghost will feel miserable because they are stuck while their loved ones have since passed and gone into the light. This is evidenced by the many EVPs I have collected where ghosts are stuck in time searching for the life they once had and the loved ones they will never find.

It is also important to mention that just because two ghosts inhabit the same place doesn't mean they are aware of each other. Even in the ghostly realm, entities are separated by vibrations and frequencies. In fact, many haunted houses are filled with discarnate entities that are completely unaware of the others that are there. Thankfully, time is experienced differently on the other side, so three hundred years may not seem as long to a ghost as it does to the living. Aside from waiting for some indefinite future event to allow the ghost to find peace, a living person can learn how to open the window of light to cross over the ghost.

People who see ghosts and spirits are able to see a higher frequency range than the average person. Many people who report seeing a ghost or deceased loved one spontaneously have done so upon waking, when they are most likely still in the theta brain wave. So don't worry if you have never seen a ghost or a spirit. With continued use of the "Road Map to the Light" technique discussed in chapter 2, you will prepare your brain to see in those higher frequencies.

When you seek to communicate with the other side, it will be important for you to know the difference between the presence of a ghost and that of a spirit. Some religions teach people that the spirit world is evil to prevent people from accessing it, and some avoid the topic all together. That approach seems to be a protective gesture from the Church and not a dismissal of the spirit world at all. When people begin to communicate with spirits, they can encounter many types of entities, including darker ones. If a person doesn't have the training to know how to discern spirits or how to cross them over, the pursuit can be harmful for them. In the following chapters, we will learn how to discern different spiritual energies and how to cross over ghosts.

4: discerning energies

Discerning spirit energy develops with practice and experience. Although you may learn many things from reading books, the best way to discern spiritual energy will stem from your ability to connect to the light. If you can connect properly, it will become easy for you to tell the difference between a residual energy (a ghost imprint), a ghost, or a spirit. You will also realize that there is nothing to fear and that you can send away any entities that are of a lower vibration.

If you have experienced a ghostly apparition, you will need to know if it is an intelligent haunting or if it is what is called a ghost imprint. Earlier, I told you about the ghost of a man that walked past my bedroom door every night. He did not communicate and did not veer from his path. He always did the same exact thing, night after night. This is an excellent example of a residual haunting, or ghost imprint. It is as if a moment in time has crisscrossed with this world and somehow remained in the environment.

This type of haunting is not intelligent, which means that the spirit is not actually trapped.

Residual Energy, or Ghost Imprints

Sometimes a person can leave a little part of themselves behind, like a recording in the environment. They are not actually still there and cannot communicate, but you may see their image. When you encounter this type of ghost, it will go about its business completely unaware of you. The ghost will always appear the same way and be doing the same thing. In this type of residual energy haunting, there is no actual ghost to cross over or soul to heal. It is the environment that needs to be cleansed of the past that it has recorded. You don't have to be dead to leave behind residual energy. The living leave traces of residual energy behind as well. I have visited places from my childhood and witnessed my own residual energy that was left behind. I have since collected it all and reclaimed it.

In some instances I have encountered a fragment of a spirit that was left behind as a ghost while the rest of them proceeded into the light. The soul was already in heaven (so to speak), but there was one small fragment that remained behind. Small fragments such as this can appear as an apparition and seem like a full ghost haunting. I have only encountered this a few times at the scenes of tragic murders. This fragment needs to be healed and released so it can rejoin the rest of the soul.

There is another type of residual haunting that affects a certain place or thing. A ghost imprint can be left behind without an actual ghost or unhealed soul. A ghost imprint is mostly composed of the energy of the living. Because everything in this world is made up of energy, we leave our mark or energy imprint on things. Sometimes an object will hold on to that energy, creating a ghost imprint, but it is not actually haunted. For instance, if you walk with a cane and use it every day for a number of years, it will most likely absorb a certain amount of your energy. When others encounter the cane, they will pick up on certain aspects of you that the cane holds as a ghost imprint. These energies should be cleared off an item before you bring it into your home. Antiques hold an enormous amount of ghost imprints, residual energy, and sometimes actual ghostly attachments, too.

Residual energy can also be experienced through your normal, everyday senses. Have you ever entered a room right after someone had an argument and noticed that the agitation was still heavy in the air? The ability to pick up on events stored energetically at a location is called *place memory*. Locations that hold strong residual energy were often the scene of a tragic event. A psychic or intuitive person who uses place memory can read the environment without any physical clues to its history. They may touch a door or wall to help pick up the transfer of energy, or they may be able to connect remotely to read a location. You may encounter a place that holds a lot of trauma and seems as if it is haunted even when it's not. It is possible to hear residual screams in an old insane asylum even if there aren't any actual ghosts haunting it. However, you will most likely find that there are ghosts trapped there—and you will want to know the difference.

Psychometry is a skill that allows a person to access psychic information about a person by touching an item they own or have come in contact with. The information is a form of residual energy that actually gets recorded onto an item. You may have seen a psychic demonstrate this skill by holding a piece of jewelry. The technique is also used quite often by psychics who work on missing persons cases. A wooden desk could hold on to the energy of the person who made it, the person who owned it, or the forest where the wood once grew as a tree. We leave our mark on everything in this world. Antique stores can be quite overwhelming for this very reason. Most items have so much history and residual energy attached to them that it can be a great place to practice your ability to feel into things. Just by holding an item, you will be able to get impressions of the people who owned it.

Ghosts

An intelligent haunting will have a ghost that attempts to alert the living people that they are present. They will usually try to get as much attention as possible by moving things, messing with your electronics, appearing as an apparition, or making noises. There are endless ways that ghosts try to communicate with the living. If you are untrained, it can seem like a lot of chaos and be very unsettling. However, most of the time, ghosts just want to be recognized and ultimately be freed from the places in which they are trapped.

The biggest difference between a spirit that is crossed and a ghost is often found in their energy frequency. For most people, energy frequency can be most easily understood as an emotional state. If the presence seems unhappy, angry, or mean-spirited, then it is most likely a ghost. If the presence appears with a wound or injury of some kind, it is most likely a ghost. If the presence is focused on revenge or any lower human emotion, it is definitely a ghost.

Ghosts are not here to comfort us. They are often confused and don't know why they are still here. Some ghosts don't realize that they are dead. Others choose not to leave because they feel the need to stay behind to look after their home, children, animals, or something else that they were very devoted to here on earth. Sometimes a ghost will simply refuse to go into the light because they are invested too much in their own ego and success here on earth and don't want to part with it.

Most of the time, ghosts are consumed by their own drama from life and want to drag you into their problems. It is not advised to pay too much attention to their perceived drama because, as we know, we all create the situations in our lives to learn from. These energies just haven't advanced enough spiritually to recognize that, and are still looking for someone else to blame. It is okay to show compassion for the ghost and help it find its way back to the light, but don't allow yourself to form energetic sympathy cords that will allow it to attach to you. If you keep a clear head about this, it will save you from ever having to worry about attachments and/or possessions.

Ghosts need to draw on the energy around them to increase their own power or life force. Therefore, ghosts don't usually thrive in abandoned buildings but prefer a sporting event or theater, where they can draw on energy from the living crowd. They can also draw energy from a full moon and a new moon. They can drain the energy from batteries and electrical appliances. When a ghost has increased energy, it is more apt to try to communicate with you. Ghosts can create disturbances in the environment around you and manipulate the temperature in the room. They can draw energy from an area of your home, which will create the infamous "cold spot." It is in the location of the cold spot that the ghost will most likely appear to you. They can also learn to move things, rattle hangers in the closet, or hide your car keys. They can touch you, run their fingers through your hair, cover you up with a blanket at night, and open and shut doors. But if the ghost is malevolent, it may shake your bed, slam doors, and try to scare you. Not all ghosts are malevolent.

Many ghosts of children will find homes to live in that have young children to play with, regardless of whether the living children are aware of their presence or not. When the living children are aware of their presence, the children often refer to them as their make-believe friends. Ghosts typically won't hurt a child directly, but their lower vibration can cause depression, scare the child, and sometimes cause illness. Recurring upper respiratory problems are common when a ghost is attached to a child. When a ghost is present, people will often "feel" a difference in temperature, indicated by a sudden chill. They may also feel distracted, short-tempered, or fatigued.

SMELLY GHOST

My husband and I encountered a ghost one afternoon while visiting a library. It became obvious to me that we were not alone, and I could feel the presence of many ghosts sitting casually in empty chairs. I asked my husband if he noticed the invisible crowd, and at just that moment, we were both overcome by a hideous and nauseating odor. We looked at each other as we covered our noses as if to silently inquire if the other had passed gas. No such luck. We didn't like the presence of the smelly ghost and decided to leave.

As soon as we got home, my husband felt ill and had to lie down. I left the room for a moment, and when I returned, the room was filled with the same odor that we had experienced at the library. My husband said he had a terrible headache and couldn't get out of bed. "Oh no! This is *not* okay with me!" I exclaimed. I knew what had happened. The smelly ghost had attached to my husband and drained his energy, making him feel instantly sick. "Get out of my house now! Go back to where you came from!" I said in a loud and firm voice, as if I had extensive military training, as I pointed my finger in the direction of the library. Immediately, the smell was completely eliminated and my husband sat up and said that his headache was gone.

CRANKY GHOST

A few years ago, my daughter experienced a ghost that affected her moods. She began acting short with everyone and withdrew from her normal activities. I wondered if it had something to do with her becoming a teenager and going through personal changes. For a week, she came home from school every day and went straight to her bedroom. She barely came out to talk or eat.

Then, on a Friday, she emerged with a smile on her face and her usual loving energy. I asked her what was wrong, and she said that she'd had an attachment. When I learned how to use the theta brain wave to connect to the light and send away unwanted entities, I taught my family how to do it as well. My daughter had noticed that she wasn't feeling quite right even though she didn't have a reason to feel the way she did. Finally, she decided to connect to the light and take a look around in the spiritual dimensions. As soon as she saw the ghostly attachment, she commanded it to go to the light. She intuitively saw an old lady's face looking back at her as she was going up into the light.

Immediately, she was back to normal! My daughter learned the Theta Healing technique when she was thirteen, and it really helped to empower her. She became more aware of what was her own emotion and what belonged to someone else.

Sometimes the ghosts we experience are the unhealed souls of our loved ones. It is a good idea to check in with your dearly departed to make sure they have gone into the light and are not hanging around on the earth plane. To do this, you will use the "Road Map to the Light" technique (see chapter 2) and ask to see and speak with your ancestor in question. Immediately, you will either feel or see the spirit as a bright soul light, or you may see no light at all. The latter is an indication that your ancestor could use some help from you to heal and cross over.

ANXIETY GHOST

One of my clients was still grieving ten years after she lost her boyfriend. She had not moved on from that moment in time. As I was working with her during a healing, I became aware that her boyfriend was still with her as a ghost who had not crossed into the light. Suddenly it all made sense. She had been feeling his unhealed emotions for the last decade and thought they were her own. She had no idea that his spirit was stuck or that the two of them needed to do some healing. I did a healing for the boyfriend and then crossed him over. Immediately, her energy shifted and she was able to receive the healing push into living in the present moment again. She no longer lived in the past, and her anxiety lessened measurably.

A ghost or other low-vibrating entity can attach to the living and create health and emotional problems for their host.

Entity Attachment

A client called to tell me about some trouble her little girl was having. It had begun a month earlier when her daughter was playing on the playground after school. She came home and told her mother that she had an imaginary friend. Her mother thought it was darling and was happy that her daughter could see ghosts. The entire family allowed the friendship to continue and often checked in to see how the invisible friend was doing. They were all under the impression that the invisible friend was a child ghost that just enjoyed hanging around the family. However, as time went on, the ghost's presence became more menacing. When the little girl didn't do what the ghost wanted her to do, it began taking things, throwing things, and threatening the girl. It was only after she got hit by the ghost that the little girl told her mother about the other bad behaviors.

While it is possible for a ghost to misbehave, it is also possible for an entity to appear as a child ghost in order to gain entry into a home. Many people feel drawn to house or parent a ghost child, and they don't realize how tricky the spirit world can be. There are other entities that will try to manipulate the living by pretending to be a ghost child. When there is hitting or threatening, you can almost always assume that it is not just a ghost you are dealing with. The entity needs to be sent into the light, and a clearing should be done on the person and property. In hindsight, the mother realized that the daughter had an ear and sinus infection that had appeared at about the same time as the invisible friend, and the girl was instantly healed after we did the clearing. Low-vibrational entities can affect the living in the same way that a ghost does.

Holy Water Bath

Many years ago, a friend called me with concerns about her four-year-old son. He had many health problems, including asthma, allergies, and drastic mood swings. Even before learning the Theta Healing technique, I was able to feel energy. Almost always when I spent time with her son, his behavior was unpredictable. It didn't seem to be triggered by a certain food or time of day. He would be fine one minute and then snap. It seemed to me that someone or something invisible was affecting him negatively.

It is difficult not being able to see what is affecting your environment, home, and the people you love. At the time, my weapon of choice was holy water. In 1995 I traveled as a spiritual pilgrim to Medjugorje, Bosnia, to experience the miracles taking place there. One night, we were told to bring our canteens of water and anything else that we wanted blessed to the church. It was known that the Virgin Mary had been appearing to several young people there for years, and each time she would bless items and heal those present. I still had my special canteen of holy water that had been blessed there. I poured some into a jar for my friend and told her to add it to her son's bath water to see if it helped him.

That night, she drew a bath like she had done every night before, and unbeknownst to her son, she poured the entire jar of holy water into his bath water. He came running when she called him and began to undress as usual. Then, as if he sensed something, he stubbornly told her that he would not get into the water. She never had to plead with her son to take a bath because it was his favorite thing to do before bedtime. However, this time, she couldn't persuade him to get into the bathtub. The more she demanded that he get in the water, the more he protested, until he began screaming and swearing at her. His mother was unprepared for his reaction, and she knew in her heart, now more than ever, how important it was to submerge his body in the holy water.

Finally, she picked him up and went to set him in the bathtub. He screamed and swore at her as his fingers and toes clung to the walls of the shower surround. Like Spider-Man, he tried to climb the walls to stay away from the water. He put up a fight with adult-level strength. This scared his mother even more, so she pushed his body into the water and held him there as he screamed bloody murder. His entire body went red, and for just a moment, she questioned if she had made the bath water too hot for him. She tested the water temperature again and found that it was the same as every other night, but she could not account for his body turning red. After the child soaked for a while, the redness faded and he became docile and well behaved again. His screaming of profanity stopped, and he began to play with his bathtub toys. This incident taught us both something. Dark entities really can attach to us, and it is possible for them to affect our health and mood.

When the bath was over, my friend put her son to bed. Things felt better in the house, and she felt a calm and peaceful energy that she hadn't experienced before. The following weeks remained peaceful, and her son didn't experience his asthma, allergies, or drastic mood swings. Something had changed.

I'm not saying that every child who is sick has something dark attached to them. I've included this story to demonstrate that this can happen. Sometimes—I stress—*sometimes* it is possible for a dark entity to attach to a living person, and the person can get physically ill from the constant energy drain. The most noticeable effect is drastic mood swings that the person seems unaware of and unable to control. Some people are more prone to this happening, and it will take regular daily work to keep clear of these entities. If you are prone to this type of spiritual attack, it will serve you to become stronger spiritually. This does not mean that you have to become religious or follow a certain religion. Becoming stronger spiritually means that you keep your vibration higher through meditation or prayer. Belief work is very helpful in changing this dynamic for a person, as are affirmations and positive thoughts.

You can pick up an entity attachment almost anywhere and not be aware of it. Having someone or something attached to you can cause a variety of problems. While they cannot make you do anything, they can affect the way you think by whispering ideas to you that influence your decisions. When someone has an entity attachment, their energy is constantly being drained. It is possible for inanimate objects to have attachments, too. Vehicles can malfunction or break down until they are cleared of the attachment.

Haunted cars, trucks, boats, and planes exist and are much more common than most people realize. Sometimes a vehicle can become haunted by its previous owner. If the owner valued and cherished their vehicle while living, it is often too difficult for them to release it in death. Some people put so much of themselves into their prized vehicle that they don't want to leave it behind. Other times a vehicle is haunted because of a death. The actual death doesn't have to have occurred in the car for the car to be haunted. A haunting could be created just by the car moving past the scene of a traffic accident. Also, when pieces are taken from a vehicle that has been involved in an accident with fatalities, those parts could create a haunting in the vehicle they are transferred to. Sometimes when a vehicle is used on paranormal investigations, a ghost or entity can attach to it. This can occur anywhere and not just at well-known haunted locations.

WATER PUMP GHOST

When I began working with a new paranormal group, they became interested in what I could do with Theta Healing. The paranormal group hosted a live broadcast each week and asked if I would be a guest on their show. Knowing how deeply personal a typical session is, we decided to conduct a session in advance so that any personal information could be edited out before airing it to the public.

The group showed up with several different cameras, microphones, and computers to monitor and record the session. As we began the healing session, the tape recorders malfunctioned and the cameras all failed. We were only able to capture a small amount of the session on film, but even that was tainted with static and wavy lines. Sometimes the very high frequency used during a healing can wreak havoc on electrical equipment.

As the crew packed up to leave my house, they mentioned that they had been having recurring issues with their truck. The water pump kept going bad, causing the truck to overheat. They needed the truck to be in good repair in order to haul all their equipment to investigation sites. I mentioned that inanimate objects could be healed and offered to do a healing on the pump to see if it helped. Either it would work or it wouldn't, and they would be no worse off. Of course, they looked at me like I was a little crazy, but they were used to dealing with the unexplainable, so they let me continue.

I laid my hand on the truck and went up to connect to the light. I commanded to remove any ghostly attachments from the truck and to send them into the light. With my eyes closed, I witnessed dark little shadows fly off and go into the light to be absorbed. Then I did a simple healing on the truck and witnessed something that seemed like it was repairing itself. When the energy finished moving, I felt like the process was done. We waved goodbye and they drove off.

Months passed, and the group asked me to appear as a guest on the show again. I was eager to have another opportunity to discuss Theta Healing and the paranormal. We were well into the live show when they told me and the entire audience that the healing on the truck had been successful. They stated that the truck had been instantly healed, without having any repair work done, and that it had remained in perfect running condition since that time!

MUSTANG LOVE

My husband purchased a Mustang convertible with the intention to resell it as an investment. He had bought it for a good price and felt that he would be able to sell it for more money than what he had paid for it. While it was listed for sale, we enjoyed driving it until a call came in from a prospective buyer. My husband panicked because he knew that something was wrong with the lights and wanted to make sure it didn't hold up the sale. The turn lights didn't work at all and hadn't worked since he had purchased the car.

The buyer planned on coming that afternoon for a test drive, so my husband had time to work on the lights. He spent the day working on the electrical panel and replacing light bulbs but found no loose wires or explanation for the malfunction. The lights just didn't work, and he didn't know why.

Finally, I told him that I would do a healing on the car to see if that would help. He needed to take a break anyway, so he let me do the healing. I sat in the car, went up to connect to the light, and commanded a healing of the car. While I was still in a meditative state, I witnessed what looked like electricity running through wires and then I cleared off any ghost energy. The entire process took about two minutes, and I went in the house to tell my husband I was finished.

My husband finished his glass of ice water and went back out to the garage. Checking the time, he knew the prospective buyer would be arriving soon. Frustrated and not knowing what else to try, he decided to turn the car on and try the lights again, just in case the healing had worked. A moment later, he ran into the house screaming like a crazy man that the car was fixed. He kept repeating himself and showed me his arms still full of goose bumps. "It worked! I can't believe it, it worked!"

The test drive went fine, and the prospective buyer purchased the car. Later, my husband confided the story of the man he had originally purchased it from. The gentleman's wife had been diagnosed with terminal cancer, and he had taken care of her as she slowly declined. She told him to do something special for himself after she passed and encouraged him to buy the muscle car that he had always wanted. After her death, he did just that and purchased the

Mustang. He kept it for a few years and processed his grief as he drove it, always thinking about her. Finally, he felt ready for a new phase of his life and decided it was time to sell the Mustang and buy something else. Had I known the story from the beginning, I would have cleared the car right away. The car served as a link for this man to his deceased wife. She loved him so much that she wanted to see his dream come true and she wanted to share it with him. She literally attached her spirit to the car in order to see it through.

I am always grateful for the way things come to us in life. If my husband hadn't bought the car, I wouldn't have done a healing on it. Did the gentleman's wife influence the sale of the Mustang to my husband because she knew it was her time to cross? Once you begin to work with the spirit world, you will be amazed at the synchronicities that spirits line up for you. They have found me in unexpected ways in an effort to get help for them and their loved ones.

Spirits

It is so common for us to experience a visit from the spirit of a deceased loved one that it is now considered natural instead of supernatural. When our loved ones die, they want to make sure that the people they left behind are okay. Grief is a process that can only be understood by those who have lived through it firsthand. Grief can take you to the deepest places within your soul as you journey toward recovery. It can make you question everything that matters in your life. When you lose someone close to you, grief can make you want to curl up and die just to be with the person you lost. The spirit world knows this and feels your grief. Spirits come back to visit to help you heal and to let you know they are okay. They often tell us that they are always around and that they are still a part of our lives. Communicating with my loved ones in spirit has given me an appreciation for life and an understanding of both life and death that I would never have had otherwise.

Put the Baby Down

My grandma told me about an experience she had with spirits when she was grieving the loss of her son. It had been three years since his death, but she was still stuck in her grief and couldn't get through the day without breaking down and crying. This type of grief can be very debilitating if it lasts a long time. This was why her loved ones in spirit came to help her through the transition.

My grandma dreamed that she was holding her son in her arms as she wept. Although he had died as a grown man, he appeared to her as an infant so that she could hold him close to her. She could feel the heat from his tiny little body as she wept. She became aware that her deceased mother and father and other family members in spirit were standing behind her with their hands on her shoulders for support. Her mother said, "Put the baby down, dear. He needs to rest now." My grandma protested and cried even harder. "I can't let him go!" Her mother said, "The baby needs to rest. It's time to put him down now." With that, my grandma slowly took the swaddled baby from her chest and set him down in a cradle.

She awoke and knew that she had experienced a visit and not just an ordinary dream. The entire day following her experience, she felt the heat of the baby against her chest. This allowed her to finally release her debilitating grief. She was able to resume going out to lunch with friends and shopping without breaking down in tears.

There are many ways that we encounter spirit visits from loved ones. These visits are referred to as after-death communication (ADC) and can occur in many different ways. The most common ADCs are sensing the presence of the deceased, hearing their voice, being physically touched, and smelling something that reminds you of them. Not everyone will be able to see the deceased as an apparition, but if you do, it will most likely occur during the in-between times of wake and sleep. The experience my grandma had occurred during her sleep state but was experienced as something very different from a dream.

It is also common to get signs that remind you of your loved one, and people have reported getting phone calls from the deceased. The spirit world knows that we long to hear from the departed, so they establish contact in whatever way that we can handle. The last thing our loved ones want to do is frighten us—so they may opt to appear through a smell or sign more often than a full-body apparition. When we get a visit from a loved one in spirit, the message is loving and healing. If their spirit has gone into the light, their message will override the negative aspects of their personality on earth. Once they shed their body, they rejoin the spirit world and merge with the light, the pure and loving energy of the Creator.

There Is No Jealousy in Heaven

My last living grandmother passed not long ago, and I began getting signs from her one week before she officially left her body. A hummingbird visited me every day and hovered in the same exact location. It started coming the moment I received notice about my grandma's failing health. My husband and I drove down to Missouri for Grandma's funeral. She had remarried, and I wanted to make sure that her new husband had love and support from Grandma's surviving family.

My grandpa had passed about ten years before Grandma, but she wasn't done living yet. Grandma stayed in her home until her failing health gave way to nursing-home living. Then, as if out of a storybook, a gentleman she had befriended playing bingo came and rescued her. They were married for only two short years, but Grandma said they were the happiest years of her life. Her funeral service was very small, because Grandma had outlived most of her friends.

As the pastor gave the eulogy, my eyes began to go out of focus. I recognized it as the time that I most often saw spirits and said mentally, "Please let me see you, Grandma. I know you are here. I can feel you." My gaze was fixed on her coffin, but I got surprised from behind with a touch. Just then, I felt a hand press on my left shoulder, as if to comfort me. It was my grandpa's hand that I felt first, and then my grandma's hand joined his. I didn't expect to be touched and immediately felt the love that my grandpa had for my grandma, and I began to cry. Up until that moment, I hadn't really cried, because I knew that my grandma had lived a good, long life. But I was so touched by the overwhelming amount of love that I felt when my grandma's and grandpa's spirits touched me.

There is no jealousy in heaven. Grandpa was happy that my grandma had found love again. I was so happy for my grandma, who had come into this world as an orphan that nobody wanted and then went out of this world being surrounded by love. I didn't hear any words from my grandparents that day, but I didn't need to. Sometimes feelings are transmitted through a simple touch.

If your desire to communicate with the other side stems from losing a loved one, you must understand that your grief can block you. The more you heal your grief, the more you become an open channel for communication. If you are feeling stuck in your grief process and are having a difficult time healing, please seek help. There are many wonderful grief support groups and a variety of different healing modalities that can help you.

Psychologists used to look at grief like, "They are dead and gone. Get over it." Well, that didn't work out so well, because nobody was able to heal from their grief. Survivors often moved on from the death of a loved one living half lives until a disease caused by broken emotions consumed them. The real issue that grieving people deal with is that the connection to their loved one is gone. It's over. They can't say they were sorry or express how much they love them. They can't just pick up the phone for a meaningless chat. It is our connection to them that we miss, and a dark, lonely abyss of empty emotions takes its place. But is the connection really gone?

Psychologists now consider it healthy to continue communicating with our loved ones after they pass. The finality of separation is healed when we accept that our loved ones are still with us in spirit. It is considered healthy—*not crazy*—to acknowledge our deceased loved ones on holidays and special occasions. Spirits of our dearly departed love to visit us and want us to be happy. When we laugh, it sends a ripple out to the spirit world, and they get to feel our happiness. But on the other hand, when we stay in grief, our loved ones on the other side don't get the opportunity to heal. Our grief can actually prevent them from ascending into the light.

A spirit that has gone into the light will vibrate at a very high frequency. Although they still retain certain personality traits, they are healed. Their personality traits help us to identify them when they come to visit. They also appear to us in a way in which we will recognize them physically. Spirits have the ability to communicate with us telepathically and don't need to say actual words to be understood. Their purpose is to express their love for us and to let us know that they still exist. Spirits can leave us signs as a special way of saying hello. Spirits can bilocate and be in more than one location at the same time. So don't worry if you feel you're hogging all of Grandma's time—her spirit can be with all of her loved ones at the same time.

Spirits can affect animals, superimpose their image onto a photograph, and make a certain song play on the radio that reminds you of them. They can make a book fall open to a page that has an important message for you to read. They can affect electrical devices of every kind, turn the radio or television on or off, make an alarm sound, or make a light bulb explode. There really is no limit to what a spirit can do when trying to get your attention. But one thing is for certain: they will never harm you in any way.

Review of the Different Energies

Let's review some differences between the energies that we may encounter.

Residual Energy, or Ghost Imprints

- May see apparition that is unresponsive to surroundings
- May hear echo of voices that are also unresponsive to questions
- Environment will hold energy that you can feel and interpret as sad, happy, etc.
- May be affected by energy that is left behind—may or may not be aware of it

Ghosts

- Gives intelligent responses to questions asked
- Can assert some type of communication
- Can move things
- Often causes electronic devices to malfunction
- Will drain batteries on investigation equipment
- Can appear as a shadow or full-body apparition
- Lower vibration can cause headaches and upper respiratory problems in the living
- Presence can cause chaos and drama with the living
- Appear as being sick, injured, or confused
- May cause cold spots in a room

- May cause goose bumps in a living person
- Will return to a place where they felt most comfortable or where they last remember being (home, bar, or where they died)
- Environment has a denser feeling than normal
- Can attach to the living and will drain their energy
- Families of unhealed spirits cannot heal from their grief
- Apparition appears to be on the same level that we are because it is earthbound
- Apparition is dull and may appear in gray tones

Spirits

- Vibration is higher, which means the spirit is healed
- Will be able to visit you in a dream and may offer a healing message
- Often manipulate the environment to deliver signs to the living
- Often cause electronic devices to malfunction
- Can move things
- Apparition is recognized by loved ones
- Tend to be most active on holidays and special occasions
- Possible for them to assist you from the other side
- Have your best interests at heart

- Presence is perceived with a warm and expansive feeling in the heart
- Can be with multiple people simultaneously (not limited to one location)
- Apparition may be slightly higher than our level and seem to float when moving

5: crossing over ghosts

Recognizing the difference between a ghost and a spirit will help you as you continue to communicate with the other side. In this chapter, you will learn a simple technique for crossing over ghosts.

By now, we have examined plenty of reasons why we should cross over ghosts that are trapped here. The next question is, how do we do that? And can anyone cross over a ghost? My answer to that last question is yes and no. Yes, anyone can learn to cross over ghosts, but not just anyone should attempt it unless they have training. If you Google "how to cross over a ghost," you will get all kinds of funky information that may or may not be useful in real circumstances. There are many ways to approach this, and I will share with you the technique I have found to be the most effective.

When you connect to the light, this connects the earth plane with the spiritual plane and it becomes easy for the ghosts that are trapped to find their way home. I am going to share the technique for crossing over ghosts through the theta brain wave. If you have practiced going into the theta brain wave by using the "Road Map to the Light" technique presented in chapter 2, this will be easy for you. Some of you may need to spend more time practicing holding the theta state, and some may need to do belief work before you can allow yourself to connect directly. Honor where you are at, and remember and know that it is our divine right to connect to the light. This technique also allows you to cross over many ghosts at the same time.

We will begin with the "Road Map to the Light" technique, and then we will insert the command to cross over ghosts.

"Crossing Over" Technique

1. Begin by sitting comfortably in a place where you will not be disturbed.

2. Close your eyes. Breathe in and out slowly to help you relax and get centered.

3. Feel the energy from Mother Earth come up through the bottoms of your feet.

4. Allow this energy to gently open each of your chakras as it rises to your crown.

5. Imagine that your consciousness goes out through your crown and above your space.

6. Continue moving your energy up until your eyelids begin to softly flutter.

7. State your intention to connect with God, Creator, or whatever your higher power is.

8. When you feel that your connection is strong, you may make this command:

   Creator, it is commanded to send any low-vibrating spirits or ghosts that are currently in this home into your light now. Heal them with your unconditional love and transform them in your light in the highest and best way now. Thank you.

9. Imagine dropping your energy down from the Creator energy and into your home.

10. Envision your house in your mind's eye.

11. Witness the process. You will see dark energies move into the light. You may see faces or feel a surge of emotions as you witness this process. It only takes a moment, and when you feel it is complete, it is. *Note: This process must be witnessed while connected to the light for it to work.*

If you are used to doing psychic work or readings, you may need to retrain yourself to connect to the light at a slightly higher level. You will definitely know the difference because you will be able to be *plugged in* and work from this level all day without getting tired. Plus, you will see how extremely fast it is to work on this level.

The "Crossing Over" technique probably seems too simple to be so powerful. Let me assure you that it really is that simple—and that powerful. Ghosts really don't belong here, and it is a universal law that they must cross over if it is commanded while being connected to Creator energy. This technique for crossing over can be used to clear many ghosts at the same time, in a moment and with ease. To demonstrate the effectiveness of this technique, I will share a real-life crossing-over experience from a paranormal investigation.

Everyone into the Light!

It was a second visit to our client's home, and we knew that we were returning in order to cross over some ghosts. The family had captured many EVPs independently of our group, and the activity had remained at a high level since the first investigation. I was fairly new to this particular group, and the lead medium didn't know how I worked. Before we entered the house, she said that she would like me to do the heavy lifting that night. That meant that she wanted me to cross over the ghosts. I was happy to take on the responsibility and agreed to do it. Then she asked me to tell her about my process, and I explained that once I make contact, I connect to the Creator and command that all wayward spirits and ghosts go into the light at once. A moment of silence passed, and then she said that she would do the crossing that night instead. Apparently, there was something different in the way we crossed over ghosts, and I was curious to witness how she worked.

There had been a lot of activity in the home, with a combination of deceased loved ones coming to visit, residual energy, and some active ghosts. On our walk-through, I detected the spirit of a young girl in the lower bedroom. The room was filled from top to bottom with antiques purchased from estate sales and auctions. Upon the mention of the little girl ghost, dried flowers began to move on their own and we heard rustling sounds in the corner. A moment later, the lead medium said that she felt the ghost touch her and pull on her dress. The energy of the little girl ghost was so palpable that we decided to leave some tape recorders running in that room.

We left the room and continued to investigate the rest of the house. About half an hour after we left the room where the little girl ghost was, we went back to retrieve the recorders. I felt that she had attached herself to a piece of china that had once belonged to her mother and that the current owners had purchased at an estate sale. We listened carefully to the recordings and were happily surprised to have captured evidence of the little girl ghost. On multiple digital recorders, we heard an EVP in a childlike voice that said, "Who are they?" and "Why are they here?"

At this point, the lead medium said she was going to cross over the little girl ghost. She began to have a conversation with her to find out why she was present and what prevented her from going into the light. Intuitively, she was answered by the ghost, and she shared that the little girl wouldn't leave because she was waiting for her dad and didn't know where he was. After several failed attempts to convince the little girl to cross over, the lead medium remarked that we couldn't help her because there was no way to know where her dad was or even what his name was. Nearly an hour passed before she decided to move on to another ghost and begin the communication process again.

The training that I received differs from many others in that I connect directly with the Creator. If a person is working strictly on the psychic level, they will need to communicate to the ghosts much in the same manner as having a conversation with a living person. If a ghost omits information or doesn't want to tell you something, they don't have to. When working on the psychic level, you are affected much more by the personality and drama of the ghosts.

What I have experienced while working in the theta brain wave is that there is no drama. The Creator knows everything, and therefore I don't have to. When I am connected to the Creator, I get the benefit of divine knowledge through the light. Crossing over becomes a simple and easy process.

With my teammates not able to help the little girl ghost, I stepped up in silence to finish the job. I was new to the group and did not want to step on the toes of any current members, so I turned my head, closed my eyes, and went up to connect to the light. Then I made this command:

Creator of All That Is, it is commanded that this little girl's father is sent to your light now in his highest and best way. Thank you.

A second later, I witnessed an energy move up into the light. When I was finished, I opened my eyes knowing that it was done. I didn't need to know who or where her father was. God knows all of that, so as I'm connected to that energy, it is done—clean and simple, with no drama. At least that was the way I was trained.

The lead medium, who was unaware of what I had done, stated that the little girl ghost was tapping her on the shoulder to get her attention again. This time, she said that the ghost stuck out her tongue and made a face at her while she pointed at me and said, "I want to talk with that lady." If I was ever unsure before of the technique I used, all doubts were instantly thrown out the window when I heard that. I immediately obliged and went back up to connect to the light. This time, I made the command to send this little girl into the light in her highest and best way and then witnessed the same process. It was amazing that the lead medium could intuitively see the ghost we were working with and knew what she was trying to communicate. I was very impressed with her mediumistic abilities, and her verification helped to solidify my crossing-over skills.

I sat quietly and waited for the lead medium to make contact and to cross over the other ghosts at the property. But after another forty-five minutes, I began to get restless. It was getting late and I had a long drive ahead of me. The ghosts were not cooperating and would not cross over. Again, I turned my head and went up to connect to the light. This time, I made this command:

Creator, it is commanded to clear this home, property, and land from any ghosts that are here. It is commanded to clear the people and things that have been affected by this lost energy and to send it all to your light in everyone's highest and best way now. Thank you.

I kept my eyes closed until I witnessed all the dark energy move into the light and up to the Creator.

When I opened my eyes a moment later, the lead medium remarked that all the ghosts were transitioning into the light. She checked on one that was especially stubborn and said that half of him was already in the light and the rest of his body was quickly fading into the light. Befuddled, she said that they must have all decided to go at once and didn't know why.

Other Ways to Cross Over Ghosts

There certainly are other ways to cross over ghosts. I prefer the technique that I learned in Theta Healing and that I shared with you because it is so fast and easy. Connecting with Creator energy allows you to work directly on the spiritual plane. It makes sense, right? Ghosts are on the spiritual plane, so it makes sense to meet them there and work with them on that level. But there is no wrong way to cross over ghosts, and I applaud anyone who feels drawn to help the spirit world in this way. Here are some other ways to cross over ghosts:

- One alternative way to cross over ghosts is to guide them to a nearby funeral home. Essentially, the ghost has chosen to stay behind and has lost their connection to the light or it is so dim that they cannot see it anymore. Some people believe that funeral homes have a light source due to the constant incoming traffic of the deceased. Remember, if the spirit is connected to the light for nine days following their death, then it makes sense that a funeral home would be a good place to find a light source. It doesn't matter that the light belongs to a recently departed person and not the ghost wandering around. The light can be used by anyone during this time frame. The light is like a one-way highway that can catapult wayward energy or ghosts back to God.

- Telling a ghost to go into the light will usually not work. They no longer have access to the light, which is why they need our help. If you are an advanced energy worker, you may be able to open portals of light that ghosts can use to cross over.

- Some ghosts are very territorial about their homes or businesses that they once loved, and they will not leave them if they are asked or told to do so. Sharing space with them may be a tolerable compromise, but understand that if you do things differently than the way they want them done, they may act up. You will have to assert yourself and let the ghost know that it is now your home/building. Command your space.

- Don't waste your time telling the ghost to go find their family. They are not connected to the light, or it is so dim that they cannot see it anymore. They cannot see the family waiting for them on the other side. For the most part, ghosts roam around in the darkness and think that our life force is the light. Prayers can be helpful, especially if they are made over a burning candle. Prayers asking Archangel Michael to usher them into the light can also be very effective.

- You may call upon the squadron of spirit helpers and former ghosts who are assigned to help in this area, to take the ghost away. You may also call upon

the angels of mercy to usher the ghosts
light.

- Make a circle by holding hands wiu.
  and, while in a meditative state, imagine ᴜ
  portal of light in the center of the circle. If everyoᴜ.
  stays focused, this will be very powerful. Once the
  ghost comes into the circle, they will immediately be
  transported up to the heavens through the light. Many
  ghosts wish to see their loved ones again and be rid of
  pain—tell them that this will help them.

- Healing yourself actually helps raise the vibration of
  a ghost, especially when the issues that need to be
  healed are what have connected you to each other.

- Sometimes performing a healing directly on a ghost
  is enough to shift it into the light and help it to cross
  over. Project love (not pity—don't buy into their
  drama) or send healing energy to the ghost. As you
  see the ghost fill up with healing light, it will merge
  with the light and go up to heaven.

- Sometimes ghosts just need to tell their story. They
  may give you signs or try to communicate the reason they are still in limbo. If you quiet yourself and
  listen, that may be enough for them, because someone knows their truth. Other ghosts may want you
  to do something for them, like solve their crime or
  find their missing body. It is not necessary for you
  to get involved in this manner, although some find
  it very fulfilling. Sometimes they just need someone

to know that they didn't kill themselves on purpose and that their death was an accident before they can move on. It is best to cross over the ghost first and then work with them in spirit to help them. Tell them that you will help them once their energy is healed in the light. This will save you time and trouble, because ghosts don't always tell the truth. Once the ghost has crossed over, they will be able to work with you in a more helpful manner.

- Burning sage can raise the vibration in a space and weaken the hold a ghost has on it, but it does not cross them over. If you find that the ghost you have is very stubborn, it is okay to use all the tools you can. Burn sage every day to weaken the energy attachment the ghost has to the location, and then cross it over.

- Often, when a person attempts to cross over a ghost, they unwittingly use their own light to do so. If you command a ghost to go into the light and the only light they see emanates from you, that is what they will use. However, many times, instead of going up to the light and crossing over, the ghost will stay in your light as an attachment. You may be completely unaware that this has happened until your health starts to suffer and you find yourself dragging, with no energy. It is always best to use the Creator's light and to witness the process as done.

Ghosts are very much caught up in their drama still, and it is from ego that they remain trapped. If you give them too much of your time, you may start living their drama. Don't forget that this is your life. You are the living, and this is your time to be here. Working with ghosts is very rewarding, but keep it in check.

FORGIVENESS CROSSES FATHER

During a healing, I connected to a deceased loved one who came in with a client. I didn't know anything about the client or her family at the time. I told her that it felt like a father energy was with her and that he appeared a bit disheveled, like an alcoholic. She got very emotional and confirmed that her father had passed and that he had indeed been an alcoholic. She was hoping that he would come through that night because she had been feeling him around her a lot. As I tapped into his energy, I intuitively saw the way he looked. I could see the way he held himself and how he dressed. I could also feel his feelings of remorse. He appeared to me in dark gray colors, which signaled to me that he had not gone into the light and that he still needed to be healed. When I described the way he appeared to me, my client knew that he needed to be healed as well.

She asked if she could have contributed to his current state because she had not forgiven him. When she left that night, she decided to call her remaining family and let them know that they all needed to forgive him in order for him to cross over into the light. Her father had created hardships for his entire family, and forgiveness was not something that came about easily. However, when they realized that they were preventing him from crossing over, they decided out of love to forgive him and release him.

This was a very special healing because each family member was released of the unforgiveness that they carried and the father was able to freely go into the light. Was it because his remorse turned into gratitude? Or was it because the act of forgiveness itself healed him? Either way, his vibration shifted and he was able to merge into the light with ease.

Being able to share the "Crossing Over" technique with you is a pleasure for me. I believe that there is a need for more people to step into these abilities right now. Ghosts have low and dull vibrations that negatively affect the living. How do you suppose millions of ghosts affect the vibration of the planet? Each and every time you help a trapped soul find the light, you participate in healing the planet energetically. You also help the loved ones of the ghost that have been suffering. The ripple effect goes out much further than you could imagine.

6: possession and oppression

The more you experience the spirit world, the more likely it is that you will encounter an entity that doesn't fit into the categories of a ghost or a spirit. There are some entities that have a darker presence, and I would be doing you a disservice if I did not teach you about darker entities and how to get rid of them, too. Although many of you will not encounter them, some of you will and it's a good idea to be prepared. The process for clearing a dark entity is just as simple as the "Crossing Over" technique, with just a slight difference: you will need to have the name of the entity in order to send it away.

It may sound impossible to acquire the name of the entity you are trying to send away, but it is actually quite simple. Sorry, thrill seekers, it is also quite uneventful most of the time. Anyone can send away dark entities safely and effectively with the use of the theta brain wave. It is my belief that the reason some exorcisms fail is because the priest is working mostly from the physical plane to push something out of the spiritual plane. I believe that priests could benefit from learning a technique such as Theta Healing in order to work with the other side more effectively. Remember, we don't have to be stronger than a dark force, because if we connect to the light, we can utilize the strength of all the heavens.

Here is the technique I use when clearing these dark energies. I always send them back to God to be transformed in the light. Be sure you don't just clear the person or location without witnessing them go back to God, or you may find yourself being attacked by them. They must leave the earth plane.

"Clearing a Demonic Entity" Technique

1. Begin by sitting comfortably in a place where you will not be disturbed.

2. Close your eyes. Breathe in and out slowly to help you relax and get centered.

3. Feel the energy from Mother Earth come up through the bottoms of your feet.

4. Allow this energy to gently open each of your chakras as it rises to your crown.

5. Imagine that your consciousness goes out through your crown and above your space.

6. Continue moving your energy up until your eyelids begin to softly flutter.

7. State your intention to connect with God, Creator, or whatever your higher power is.

8. When you feel that your connection is strong, you may make this command:

Creator, it is commanded to know the name of this entity now.

You will hear or intuitively know the name immediately. Then say:

Creator, it is commanded to take (use the name you were given) into your light now. Thank you.

9. Imagine dropping your energy down from the Creator energy and into the place from which you wish to send the entity away. This includes the body of a person who is currently a host to a demonic entity.

10. Envision the place/person in your mind's eye.

11. Witness the process. You will see dark energies move into the light. Wait for the process to be complete. Make sure the entity is all the way up into the light, and then imagine slamming a door to keep it from returning. *Note: This process must be witnessed while connected to the light for it to work.*

Dark entities can reside in any location and within a person. When you come upon a haunting that seems especially dark, it may have a demonic entity present. If the living people are being scratched, seeing glowing red eyes, hearing grunts or growls, or feeling threatened, it is most likely a demonic entity. The first rule of thumb is to do a normal crossing over for any ghosts that are trapped in the location. This will narrow down the spirits that you are working with. If it is a menacing ghost and not a demon, it will leave with the "Crossing Over" technique. If it doesn't leave and you feel that the presence wants to harm you, then use the "Clearing a Demonic Entity" technique. If you call the entity by name while being connected to the Creator, it must go.

There are some people who say that possession is not real. Perhaps they feel that way because they have not personally experienced one. It seems foolish and naive to limit the other side and expect the spirit world to follow the guidelines of black and white. Consider the entire spirit world a gray area where things will happen even years after you've formed your thoughts and beliefs about what you understand. Human beings like to figure things out so we can feel a sense of security. However, the spirit world is made up of endless possibilities that will shake you up and teach you something new each time you get involved.

Dark entities may appear in the form of an angry ghost, a creature, or a demon. But they can also masquerade as a seemingly harmless child ghost or one that you would typically welcome. They are very manipulative and will attempt to trick you in order to gain power. Whether or not the dark entity takes on the form of a ghost doesn't matter. The important thing is for you to know that they are real so that you will be well prepared to extinguish them if you encounter them. Just as there are good and bad people who are living, there are good and bad entities that exist in the spirit world.

When I traveled to Medjugorje, a healing priest accompanied us on the trip. He worked with everyone who was open to learning and taught us for three days how to heal and eliminate dark entities. I was curious about why he wanted to teach average laypeople to do the type of healing he did, and he told me that there was a great need for healing on our planet and too few healing priests. He said that we all needed to learn how to heal ourselves and others. His words changed my life that day because I finally had the permission I had sought to do the work I felt called to do.

The priest told us to command to know the demon's name when working with dark entities. He also said that we could cast the entity away by exclaiming the words "blood of Christ." The words themselves were extremely powerful, he said. Over the years, I used what the healing priest taught me with impressive results. I also learned every other method of clearing spirits and working with energy that I could so that I was well prepared. By the time I learned the technique through Theta Healing, it seemed I had come full circle. The techniques are similar, with the main difference being that the Theta Healing technique uses a slower brain wave, which allows me to witness the clearing on the spiritual plane.

Healing from Attack

Every home I have lived in as an adult has had a special healing room in it. People seeking healing usually find me through friends or past clients. One day, a young woman came to see me for a healing, but she wouldn't share with me what was wrong. I found out later that it was sort of a test, because she had already been to many different healers without success.

At the time she came to see me, I was living with a friend who was a massage therapist and my five-year-old daughter. I asked my roommate to help with this healing. We lit a candle and began to work energetically with the woman as we prayed. At first it didn't seem like anything was happening, and then I remembered what the healing priest had taught me. The flame on the candle suddenly expanded to a height of twelve inches as it flickered and jumped above the wick. We both noticed this and knew that something big was about to happen. My daughter came over and joined in our efforts, sending our client love.

Suddenly, as if it had been building up for a lifetime, the energy in the room felt like an explosion. Our client began to wail in agony as she curled her body into a fetal position. She contorted and convulsed for a few minutes and then finally simmered into a soft and delicate cry. When she was able to speak to us, she told us that she had been the victim of a gang rape many years prior. She had been seeking healing but confessed that none of the healers had been able to get deep enough to help her release the pain.

Many times when a person has been a victim of a violent attack, the demon that influenced the attacker actually takes up residence in the victim. It's as if it jumps from one host to another. At times, the victim is emotionally and spiritually shattered, which leaves them weak and open for the entity to enter. The energetic healing in this case helped to open our client up and prepare her for what was about to leave. But the words I muttered, "blood of Christ," catapulted the demon out of her. Months later, I saw her and she was like a new person. She had made many changes in her life and was joyous again.

FAINTING LOUNGE

I was working with a client one day and became aware that she had a nasty entity inside her. She had been diagnosed with mental health problems and prescribed some pretty heavy medications. She said that she was unable to connect to God and, after many failed attempts, called me for help.

Medication can impair a person's ability to connect with the light. But in this woman's case, she had become a host body for a very dark entity. When

I realized what the situation was, I reflected back on my earlier training in dealing with dark spirits. Everything the healing priest had taught me and everything I had learned in Theta Healing melded together. I was reassured that the technique I was using was effective and proceeded with the healing.

With my poker face on, so as not to alarm my client, I asked if I could clear some negative energy from her. She agreed. I connected to the light and silently commanded to know the demon's name. Intuitively, I received a name right away. In my head, I called it by name and commanded it to go back to God. I then witnessed the dark shadow go up in the highway of light and imagined slamming the door to heaven shut. It's God's law—when you command an entity to go while being connected to the light, it must go. When I knew the process was done, I opened my eyes and continued working on my client's beliefs.

She abruptly backed away from me and said that she needed to lie down. She asked for juice or something to drink as she physically collapsed onto the fainting lounge in my healing room. I didn't tell her I had removed a dark spirit that had possessed her because she would have been consumed with fear. But it was very interesting to see how her body was affected by the removal of one so powerful.

That was my first experience clearing a possession by using the technique I learned in Theta Healing. I have encountered several other possessions since that time and have cleared them with the same level of ease and effectiveness. In doing this type of clearing, it may be more common to come across an oppression rather than a full possession.

Personal Demons

Many years ago, I experienced something that changed the way I perceived evil. It seemed like I was living through a battle between good and evil, and the partner in my life at that time had his own demons to deal with. For some people, personal demons may be issues of physical abuse, drugs, or alcohol. Of course, I thought I could help him by loving him enough, but he was pretty broken and set in his ways. I decided to attend a healing Mass so that I could heal the part of me that kept attracting the same type of man. My partner came with me, but when it was my turn for the healing, he barged onto the altar, stood beside me, and asked them to heal our relationship instead. I was mortified, but I bowed my head for the group to pray over us anyway.

As the group was praying over us, I began to feel sharp fingernails crawl up my spine. With my head bowed, I actually saw my heavy-knit sweater lift as an invisible creature crawled out of me. I was terrified to know that something like that had been inside of me. The healer told me that I had quite literally taken that on for someone I loved. She said to fill myself up with love immediately so it could not return.

Some people think that possession is a cop-out for someone who doesn't want to own up to the bad things they've done. But I believe that people are possessed much more often than we are aware of and that our prisons are full of people who have experienced the phenomenon. However, that does not remove responsibility from what I call the "body host." The body host is still responsible for allowing their spiritual body to become so weak that it was easy for an entity to enter them.

How does someone become weak spiritually? Just as a spirit can choose the light or turn away from it, living people make that choice, too. Every day, we are confronted with ethical decisions that either help us to strengthen our spirit or weaken it. When we lie, our spirit grows weak. When we intentionally hurt someone, our spirit grows weak. Alternately, truth is a powerful force and always strengthens the spirit. Helping someone to heal (including yourself) strengthens your spirit.

In terms of spiritual energy, we have to think of other people as part of ourselves. We really are connected to everyone around us at all times on both sides of the veil. Many times, a person wants to do good things and live a good life, but they feel beaten down by their surroundings.

Often the abused child grows into the abusive parent. No matter how hard they try to behave differently, their subconscious programs bring them back to abuse. These subconscious programs can be changed and healed. No matter what harm was done to you as a child, you can seek healing and change the course of your life if you choose to.

When a person has lived life and habitually made choices that were harmful to others, their spirit becomes weak and their light becomes dim. When this happens to a living person, it becomes very easy for low-vibrational entities to take up residence within them. It could also happen through a lengthy illness where a person gives up hope or when someone subjects their body to drugs and excessive alcohol. There are some people who are vibrating so low spiritually that they actually feel soulless. They have a blank and lackluster look in their eyes and are the spiritual equivalent of the walking dead. These people make excellent host bodies for dark entities to inhabit.

Sometimes a person wishes to be spiritually strong but is filled with fear of dark forces. This usually is the result of an overly religious upbringing that was meant to serve the individual but that actually weakened them through fear. Fear is a very low vibration, and I believe it is up to us to face our fears in order to learn and grow.

A dark entity can affect living people in the environment it occupies or it can affect the living more directly through oppression and possession.

Oppression

Oppression is where a dark entity or ghost tries to break you down slowly so that it can possess you. Here are some classic symptoms of oppression:

- Compulsive thoughts and feelings

- Extremely low self-image

- Constant confusion

- Inability to believe in God (or hope or goodness)

- Perceiving anger or hostility in others when it doesn't really exist

- Nightmares that may have demonic images

- Violent thoughts (suicidal, homicidal, encouraging self-abuse, etc.)

- Tremendous hostility or fear when encountering someone involved with deliverance work—this can be someone who removes evil spirits or who frees those held in the bondage of the evil spirit

- Deep depression and despondency

- Irrational fears, panic attacks, and phobias

- Irrational anger and rage

- Irrational guilt and self-condemnation

- A desire to do what is right with an inability to carry it out

- Sudden personality and attitude changes

- Compulsive behaviors

- A strong aversion to God

- Hollow look in eyes with contraction of the pupils
- Lying, exaggerating, or stealing
- Compulsive sex
- Eating obsessions (including bulimia and anorexia nervosa)
- Irrational laughter or crying
- Facial features contort or change
- Inability to look at you in the eyes
- Drug abuse (especially when there are demonic hallucinations)
- Compulsion to hurt oneself and others
- Sudden speaking of a language not previously known
- Verbal or body-language reactions to the name and blood of Jesus
- Extreme restlessness (especially in a spiritual environment)
- Uncontrollable cutting and mocking tongue
- Vulgar language and actions
- Consciousness problems
- Loss of time (from minutes to hours—ending up someplace without knowing how you got there, regularly doing things of which you have no memory, etc.)
- Extreme sleepiness around spiritual things
- Demonstration of extraordinary abilities that appeared suddenly

- Voices are heard in the mind (they mock, intimidate, accuse, threaten, or bargain)
- Subject refers to him/herself in the third person
- Abnormal medical problems
- Seizures
- Blackouts
- Pain (without justifiable explanation—especially in the head and/or stomach)
- Physical ailments that can often be alleviated immediately by a command of spiritual authority
- Sudden buzzing in ears, inability to speak or hear, severe headache, heightened sensitivity to noise or touch, chills or overwhelming body heat, numbness in arms or legs, and even temporary paralysis

It is not necessary to have all these symptoms, but to a trained eye or someone who works with such energies, it will be quite obvious.

If you think that you or someone close to you is experiencing oppression, it is important to get help. This is a spiritual matter and will not go away until it is treated on the spiritual level. It will be difficult for a person who is being oppressed to reach out, because the entity will not want to be sent away. They will say whatever they need to in order to stay around.

Sometimes people who are very open psychically can be attacked by a dark entity. It is important to understand that when you are very open, you must take more responsibility to grow spiritually and learn to protect yourself from lower energies. Oftentimes people reopen to their natural psychic abilities when they reach maturity. In most cases, this would be around age forty.

DEMON MAGNET

My husband used to be affected by dark entities on a regular basis and would drag them home with him. It was obvious to my daughter and me, because he would literally look like a different man and behave negatively. I gave him the Archangel Michael prayer and told him to say it in his car before he came in the house after being away. On the occasions that he forgot to say the prayer and clear off his energy, we had major unexplained disruptions in the house.

One time, he came in late at night after finishing a construction job. As he showered, he remembered that he had forgotten to say the prayer, so he did it while he was in the shower. Not thinking twice about it, he got out quietly and came to bed. A moment later, we heard the water turn back on by itself. The shower head fell from the wall mount, and all the shampoo and conditioner bottles fell off the shelf and landed with a huge thud! I asked him if he had remembered to clear off before he came home and he admitted that he had done it in the shower.

There was an incident involving my husband that happened when we first began to date. Following his divorce, he temporarily lived at his parents' house. He was sleeping in the guest room and was awakened when he felt someone or something sit down on the foot of the bed. Out of reflex, he kicked his legs and then opened his eyes to look around. The ceiling of the room had black shadow figures swirling around over the bed. He was terrified and didn't know how to protect himself. Since that time, we have learned a lot about protection and how important it is to empower yourself through prayer and meditation.

My husband has learned how to keep his energy balanced and protected through meditation, healing, and clearing off. We no longer experience these types of disruptions, and you can learn how to do this for yourself, too.

To overcome spirit oppression, you must take a stand. You should raise your vibration through whatever means possible, such as diet, exercise, no drugs, no alcohol, forgiveness work, overcoming fear, sea salt baths, saging your home, listening to uplifting music, and watching whom you surround yourself with. You should look for friends who have a positive outlook and a higher vibration—this is no time for Debbie Downers or Poor Me's! You may also connect to the light through meditation or prayer and/or see a healer or spiritual advisor who can help you. Once you lick this problem, you shouldn't have any more trouble. You won't be any fun to mess with once you empower yourself!

Possession

In order for a person to be possessed, they have to allow a spirit or entity to take control of them. You must interact with the entity and encourage it to stay and spend time with you rather than send it away. In essence, you must invite them in for them to be able to possess you. As a living person, you have the authority to protect yourself. A spirit or entity cannot stay in a living body unless it was invited. Never, under any circumstances, allow a spirit to enter your body.

7: types of hauntings

If you desire to learn more about ghosts and don't currently live in a haunted house, you will need to locate places that have paranormal activity. You shouldn't need to travel far to find one, because they exist all over. In this chapter, I will give you tips on where to find a haunted location near you. Reported hauntings have increased dramatically in recent years, which should make it easy for you to find some. But are there really more ghosts, or are there simply more people experiencing ghosts because of all the readily available paranormal devices? In the past, people relied solely on visual contact of a ghost. We now have devices that help us validate the phenomenon of a haunting, which allows the general public to have access to a world they once were denied.

Consciousness has shifted within the general public as well. It is more acceptable to discuss ghosts, and more people are sharing the experiences they have had. Does this have something to do with the earth's vibrational changes, which have literally dropped the veil between worlds? The veil is an imagined thing that separates us from the other side. More accurately, it is the separation of vibrations between planes. Are there really more dead people that are choosing not to go into the light these days, or are we just more aware of them?

I can't form an argument that suggests that death was any more tragic in one era than another. Ancient tribes suffered terrible deaths from battle, human sacrifice, and starvation. There were plagues that ravaged whole towns and natural disasters that took hundreds of lives at once. There were murders, suicides, car accidents, health problems, drownings, and countless other ways that people experienced death. But no matter how a person dies, the living are always affected. It makes no difference what nationality or race a person is. We all share in the human experience of death and the loss of loved ones. There will always be the accompanying emotions that go with the loss of life, such as grief and the feeling of having unfinished business.

What determines if a person will transition easily into the light or stay behind and be witnessed as a ghost? Does the choice depend on the injustice of the death? The brutality? Or the timing of when it occurred? All these factors contribute to the choice to stay behind, but ultimately, it is a matter of our own *free will*. That means that we are just as likely to encounter a ghost who died in a freak accident as one who died of old age.

Many people who decide to work with the spirit world seem to be chosen by the other side. These are people who have had repeated experiences with the spirit world throughout their lives and who cannot ignore the call to help. Those people won't need to go looking for ghosts, because the ghosts will find them. But they will need to learn how to discern spirits, protect themselves, and cross over ghosts. Once you have applied the techniques in this book to help ghosts heal and move into the light, the process will become second nature. You may find yourself doing this work professionally or as part of your daily routine.

To better your chances of finding a lost soul, it makes sense to go to a place where many of them perished. Every area has something in its history that would be significant to a ghost enthusiast. Research the town you live in to find out if any trains derailed, gold mines caved in, or planes crashed. Wherever there has been a tragedy responsible for taking many lives, the chances will be good for finding ghosts. If your town or city has legends of haunted places, that may be a good place to start. Ghosts have always been a part of the invisible landscape that surrounds us, and now you will be able to communicate with them.

Haunted Locations

Hospitals

Hospitals are places where deaths occur frequently, and most towns have one. Obviously, you would not tramp through the halls with your paranormal equipment at a functional hospital. But if the building is vacant or used for another purpose now, you may be able to investigate it. You do not have to be inside a haunted property in order to communicate with ghosts. If you come anywhere near their vicinity, they will find you.

Nursing Homes

As people get older and lose the ability to care for themselves, they frequently move into nursing homes. This type of facility nurtures people who are nearing the end of their lives. Eventually, everyone at the nursing home will pass and move into the spirit world. This is a normal and natural phase of life during which many people wait out their final days, doing life reviews and preparing for death. Sometimes when people reach this stage of pre-death, they are on many medications. Some medications can affect a person's faculties and, at times, interfere with the natural crossing-over process. Again, this is not a location that can be investigated while it is operable. As with a hospital, any active nursing home will need to be investigated from a distance. What you should look for is an abandoned facility that was once used in this capacity. An old, abandoned hospital or nursing home is very likely to be the host of active hauntings.

Funeral Homes

Funeral homes serve as a gathering place for the newly departed and bereaved. This type of business is always active because of the amount of high human emotion and recent loss of life. Funeral homes are said to be great sources of light because they house all the recent deaths where spirits still retain connection to their light source. Ghosts may utilize another spirit's light source as a way of crossing over if they have lost their own connection. I believe that most people stay behind after death to attend their own funeral before going into the light. Once the funeral service is over and the family goes back home, some spirits stay behind out of confusion. This means that a funeral home may be filled to the brim with ghosts and spirits on any given day.

Cemetery

There are some who say that ghosts don't hang out at cemeteries because they prefer locations with lots of people and energy. However, I have yet to visit a cemetery where I did not capture an intelligent response on EVP. It doesn't matter if the cemetery is old or new, active or abandoned. If you choose to do paranormal investigating at a cemetery, please follow guidelines and be respectful! While this work is exciting for you, consider that anyone else you encounter there will be mourning. How would you feel if you were at the grave of a recently departed loved one and some yahoos came running along with investigation devices? When I go to a cemetery, I do it very discreetly, and my purpose is to see if there are any ghosts that need to be crossed. It has been my personal experience that there is a lot of activity at and near cemeteries.

OVER GROVER

Once I visited a historic cemetery with a paranormal investigation team to see if there were any ghosts that needed help. After being drawn to a certain section designated for war veterans, we began to feel light-headed and dizzy. We asked if there was anyone with us and if they had anything to say. We ran the recorder for only one minute, but we knew we had captured an EVP because we felt the ghost energy so strongly. When we reviewed the recording, we heard in a scratchy male voice, "We don't want no over grover here, damn it." We were thrilled to find the EVP but had no idea what it meant.

It took a little research to find out what "over grover" meant. We searched the time period of the headstones that were around us and discovered that the president of the United States was Grover Cleveland. He was the only United States president to run for office in two nonconsecutive terms. Everyone loved him during his first term. Then, during his second term, the country had massive economic problems and everyone turned against him, saying things like, "We are over Grover." If you like history, you will really enjoy some of the things ghosts teach you. This ghost was a military vet who served proudly and couldn't stand the people who had turned against the leader of his country.

Schools

Many times, schools are haunted. Sometimes school was a happy place for a child and they want to stay behind after they die to play with their friends. Other students return out of habit, not even knowing they have passed. Students of higher learning may return out of dedication to their education and not know how to give up their desire to work toward their profession or dream. Public schools tend to be active, and it is likely that they will attract any child ghost that can see and hear the living children who are there. Places that are supercharged with the joy of children can be highly appealing to ghosts.

Theaters

"The show must go on" applies to theaters that operate with a full living cast along with a ghostly ensemble. Theaters attract audiences of all kinds seeking entertainment, music, and plays. Sometimes theaters are haunted by people who died and who loved going to the theater in life. Other times theaters are haunted by the cast and crew who couldn't give up the stage after death because they long for another performance or chance to be in the limelight. This type of haunting could apply to a movie theater or an old-fashioned stage theater. Both types invoke the same human emotions and energy that ghosts need to thrive.

Library

Libraries are wonderful places to gain access to the spirit world. Think about all the books that people take into their own homes and then return to the library. It is easy for a book to get a ghostly attachment and then end up at the library. It could also work the other way around. Sometimes ghosts love the library because it offers them access to the public. Many ghosts that are enthusiastic about certain topics will attach themselves to a book covering the same information that will appeal to the like-minded living. Libraries often have research areas and house old photographs, microfilm, and historic information about the town. This often appeals to a ghost that is trapped in time and can't let go of their history in order to move on.

Hotels

Hotels of all kinds are known to be paranormal hot spots. Sometimes the hotel has experienced the death of patrons, but it doesn't have to have a death to be haunted. The people who travel and stay at hotels come with their own baggage, both physical and supernatural. The energy is constantly turned over and can serve as a cesspool of activity. Lots of human emotions gather there, and ghosts can easily feed off that environment.

Historic Buildings

Historic buildings of all kinds seem to hold pieces of the past in the form of ghostly inhabitants. These can often be felt by people who are otherwise unaware of ghosts. They may not know what it is but will comment about feeling creeped out or completely at home in the location. There is often a heaviness felt in the air and emotions that linger and affect the living. When you are suddenly overcome by a change in emotion that doesn't seem to make sense, it may actually be the emotions of a ghost you are feeling. Being able to feel someone else's emotions means that you are an empath. An empath will often think they are feeling something that they have actually absorbed from someone around them—it could be from the living or the dead. That's why it's important for an empathic person to protect their energy and regularly clear their energy field. Protection techniques will be covered in detail in chapter 13.

Bars

It should go without saying that bars are active with spirit energy and make excellent places to conduct paranormal investigations. Sometimes a ghost will return to a place where they spent a lot of time when they were living. The comfortable seat at the end of the bar where they visited with friends each night after work can make such an impact that they return there after they die. For many, a bar served as the only place where they felt a sense of family or community. They love that it fills up with people each night, and they sometimes take the opportunity to influence the living who have become good candidates for attachments. When a person drinks alcohol, they often lose the ability to protect themselves from entities. This creates a playground for the supernatural, and spirits are magnetically drawn to it. I am not saying that you should stay away from bars. I love to meet friends for drinks, and bars are a great place to socialize. What I am suggesting is that you should pay attention to the way you feel and make sure to clear off your energy before you get home. I will teach you how to do this in chapter 13.

Insane Asylums

Most insane asylums were closed down in the 1970s due to their horrific living conditions. For the most part, they were drastically understaffed and filled to overcapacity with people with mental illnesses. If you decide to investigate at an old asylum, you should be prepared to encounter ghosts that still seem to be mentally ill, as well as many dark entities. Most people who have a mental illness make an excellent host for dark entities, and the two often appear together. You will have to be on your toes as you investigate this type of facility. Some insane asylums still sit empty and abandoned, while others have been turned into nursing homes or other state-run facilities. I know of one building that served as both and is now a hotel!

STOWAWAYS

One day my daughter and I were on an impromptu investigation at the location of an old insane asylum. The original structure had been torn down and replaced by a newer building that housed the elderly. We decided to be discreet and conduct our investigation on the grounds behind the facility. There were still many original outbuildings that had been used to harvest food for the asylum. At one time it had functioned as a farm that could sustain itself for the residents' meals. I couldn't tune out the intuitive images I had of people running around the lawn wearing white gowns. We were inexplicably drawn to an area covered by tall trees. As we entered, my daughter began to feel pressure in her head and tingling sensations throughout her body. She expressed how dizzy she felt and asked how I was feeling. All I wanted to do was run around and spin in circles with everyone else. I felt like twirling with my arms outstretched. We laughed as we compared the different experiences we were having. The ghost that she had come into contact with was definitely sedated with heavy medication, while the one that I had connected with was feeling higher than a kite!

We wanted to help the ghosts, but our visit was cut short by the security team who had found our car and awaited our return. They were actually quite friendly and offered us historical information about the property. It was their job to secure the area to make sure people didn't get hurt in the old buildings. We completely understood and headed out rather quickly. When my daughter and I pulled into our driveway, she reminded me that we hadn't cleared off our energy. Oops! At that moment, we both realized that our car was filled with countless stowaways from the facility. Their expressions were influenced by the heavy drugs they had been administered in life, which made them look distorted, but their behavior was childlike and silly. We let them out on the lawn and told them they had a few hours to run around before we would cross them over. All afternoon, we were affected by their energy, and I still wanted to spin in circles. When it was time, we crossed all the ghosts into the light, and the yard returned to its natural state. It was quite an experience that still makes me laugh when I think about it.

Grocery Store

A super common place for ghosts to hang out is in the grocery store. There are plenty of living people who visit there each day. Many ghosts wore a daily path to the grocery store when they were living, and they may even enjoy seeing the friendly faces that used to greet them.

The best way to determine if a ghost is following you around the store is to be observant. I have literally had things fly off the shelf and arc in midair when a ghost or spirit was present. I have even had deceased loved ones come with me to shop in order to get my attention.

HAPPY BIRTHDAY, GRANDPA!

Recently, I experienced a visit from a loved one when I went shopping to pick up dinner. The fresh produce was in the front of the store, and I headed straight in that direction. I noticed that my energy seemed extra big as I walked past other shoppers. There were a few people with parked shopping carts in front of the produce as they squeezed and smelled for freshness. Just as I came near, an older woman placed her selection in the cart and turned to leave. I don't know what made me notice this, but I watched the woman and saw the head of lettuce jump off the shelf and roll in front of her cart. The woman was slightly embarrassed as she picked it up and placed it back on the shelf. She wasn't close enough to the produce shelf to have bumped it. She noticed me looking at her and I said, "Looks like you got a jumper." She laughed and nodded and then walked off in the other direction.

Moments later, I witnessed the same thing happen to a young woman who was standing about ten feet away from the first. This time, a bag of carrots jumped off the shelf and landed at her feet. Knowing that she had heard me the first time, I repeated my comment, "Looks like you have a jumper, too." She looked puzzled as she picked up the carrots and returned them to the shelf. I wasn't quite sure who wanted to be noticed, but I figured I had better get out of the produce aisle until those women left.

When I returned home, I called my sister and told her what had happened. I told her that I hadn't checked in to see who it was but that I knew it was someone for me. She said, "It feels like Grandpa." And just as the words left her mouth, a large "Happy Birthday" sign fell off my wall and brushed the back of my hair as it fell. With that mention, we knew instantly which grandpa it was because it was his birthday.

Spirits love to be remembered on special days and holidays. My grandpa's spirit was able to use the food to get my attention at the store. Once that happened, I was alerted to pay attention to find out who was with me. We had celebrated some other family birthdays earlier in the month and still had our decorations hanging in place. It was pretty easy for my grandpa to knock the sign off the wall in order to confirm his presence.

Shower

Many people experience visits from the spirit world while they shower. This is actually quite normal, and there are several contributing factors. First, you are enclosed in a small space similar to the size of what the spiritualists use as a cabinet in mediumship. The energy tends to build in a small space, making it easier for spirit communication to take place. Second, water is a conductor of energy, so this helps bridge the gap energetically between the physical and spiritual dimensions. Third, whenever you do something repetitively, your brain naturally slips into a slower theta brain wave. Most people don't have to think about how to wash their hair or shave their legs, and they typically perform these tasks on autopilot while their mind wanders. This mental state is the one in which we are most receptive to receiving messages from the spirit world. I often get visits in the shower from deceased loved ones. At times I also get visits from unfamiliar spirits that want me to give a message to their living loved ones whom I know. There is nothing crude about being visited in the shower. It is probably just the best set of circumstances for spirits to make contact with us.

Spirit in the Shower

I connected with a friend's father who had passed to see if he had a message for his son, whom I was meeting later that day. I wrote down everything he told me. As I headed off to shower, I mentally told his father "thank you" and to let me know if there was anything else he needed to say to his son.

A few minutes later, I was in the shower shaving my legs when I literally saw an energy move into the shower with me. The energy swirled around by my head, and then I heard the word "syndicate." I was dumbfounded—what did that mean? Then I heard it again, "syndicate." I knew the word but wasn't quite clear about what it meant. I decided to look up the word on my computer when I finished my shower. My mind was still whirling as I wondered what needed to be syndicated. Immediately, I saw in my mind's eye what appeared to be a broadcast logo. It was a triangle-shape image with a tall, narrow top and had circles coming out from the top of the point. As soon as I asked myself what that image was, I heard the word "broadcast." Okay, now I thought I got it. Even though I wasn't quite sure what it meant to syndicate a broadcast, I knew that this was a message for my friend.

Later that evening, I overheard my friend tell someone that he wanted to syndicate his broadcast. I hadn't told him yet what had happened to me earlier in the day. I was so amazed and knew in my heart that his dad had visited me and wanted me to give him that message. I believe his father was validating something that his son was working on at the time as a way to show him that he was still around. He thought it was a great idea and wanted to support his son to take the next big step in his career.

Children and Animals

Child Ghosts

Child ghosts can be a very touchy subject. What person wants to believe that God would allow a child to be trapped as a ghost? This leads us back to a broader perspective of how the spirit world operates. What if God is not some omnipotent parent-like figure that religions have made him out to be? What if the Creator of All That Is actually is completely unbiased and allows each soul equal opportunity to have free will? What age would be considered old enough to choose the light or to turn away from it? Do chronological years add depth to a child's soul?

I personally have not experienced a ghost under the age of four or five. While I have heard the faint echo of a baby's cry, it was a residual ghost imprint rather than an actual ghost. Babies are unfiltered by fear, regret, and unforgiveness, so their light is the strongest on the planet. When a baby or small child dies, they are absorbed directly back into the light. They may be accompanied by guardian angels that specialize in the transition of precious little souls.

Though the thought of it makes most people gasp in terror, some religions believe that original sin can condemn even a fetus to hell. With respect to many different religions and belief systems, my beliefs differ. I do believe that we carry the sins of our ancestors in our DNA. Therefore, the unhealed issues of the mother and father do affect an unborn child. However, even if a growing fetus absorbs hate and fear from the parents, it still has a powerful connection to the Creator. If the baby's frequency is vibrating high enough, it should be able to enter the light immediately upon passing, no questions asked.

Angels and Saints for Babies

When calling upon help from the spirit world, you can borrow ascended masters from any religion. They all have their own specialties and aren't confined to any particular belief system.

Saint Gerard Majella is the patron saint of expectant mothers. Saint Gerard had the mystical ability to levitate and bilocate. He is often prayed to during a difficult pregnancy and is considered the patron saint of motherhood.

Gabriel is the angel of annunciation and resurrection. Gabriel is known as the messenger of God and will help those who wish to work with children. Gabriel is known to assist with all aspects of parenting, along with conception, adoption, and birth.

Temeluch is an angel responsible for pregnancy and assists Gabriel in instructing the unborn baby in utero. He looks after newborns and children as well. Temeluch is a guardian angel and a childbed angel who watches over the little ones and keeps them safe from dark entities.

Everyone has their own guardian angels that are assigned to them from the moment of conception. There is no limit to how many angels you can call upon. Each time you pray for help from an angel, another one joins your team of spirit helpers. Your angelic team grows throughout your life. However, you must ask them for assistance, because they cannot intervene without it. This angelic energy can help us vibrate in love, which allows us to forgive more easily and heal faster. If you ever encounter a baby or child ghost, don't hesitate to call on one of these spiritual child advocates for help.

Miscarriage

While I have not experienced a baby ghost, I have come across the spirits of miscarried babies that have chosen to stay beside their mother. When I do an intuitive body scan, I can often see if the mother has experienced the loss of a baby. Their spirit light tends to be very close to the mother and hover around the lower part of her body.

Baby Guides

I was working at a Holistic Expo when an older woman sat down with me and asked for a mini healing session. Taking her hands in mine, I went up to connect to the light. As I scanned her body, I became aware that there were two little lights shining beside her upper thigh area. Immediately, I felt they were little children. She confirmed that she had lost two babies to miscarriage, but that it had been a long time ago. I informed her that her babies were still with her in spirit.

When I connected with the energy of the babies, I was told that they had needed a way to get here (onto the earth plane) but that they didn't need a physical body to do what they came here to do. Their help was always meant to be from the spirit world, and they came to be guides for their mama. Sometimes I still get surprised when I hear things like that, but it resonated with truth. I shared the message with the woman, who began to sob. She had been carrying the grief for decades, and she was never able to conceive again. It was healing and magical for her to realize that God had not punished her and that she was being loved and guided all along by her babies in spirit.

Aborted Babies

I have also seen the energy of aborted babies hanging around the mother, but their energy is not healed like the spirit babies that are the result of a miscarriage. This is just an observation from what I have seen and not a judgment in any way. In the case of an abortion, essentially there was a choice to end the pregnancy. It does not matter if the mother was forced into making the decision or if she made it willingly. The energy involved is that the baby was not wanted, and that creates a spiritual wound. Both men and women are affected by this choice spiritually and energetically. If you think about a baby that is wanted, the energy is love, anticipation, and excitement. These high-vibrational emotions energetically affect the DNA of the fetus and affect the life and health of the baby. But in a case where the opposite is true and the baby is unwanted, those emotions also affect the soul of the baby.

The good news is that there is a special healing you can do to help heal aborted babies by sending them the love they didn't receive. I became aware of this issue while working within the spiritual dimensions. Many of my clients have shared that they have been affected spiritually by this choice, sometimes decades later. The healing benefits of this technique make a difference in the living as well. Everyone connected to the DNA of the fetus will receive a healing spiritually when this takes place.

Many times, the aborted baby hangs around the mother until she conceives again. Although the father is affected on a spiritual level, I have only seen the baby follow the mother to attempt reentry through her next pregnancy. It is entirely possible that the unhealed spirit baby follows both parents around; I have just not experienced this yet. If the spirit of the aborted baby remains unhealed, the imbalance can cause the new baby to be sickly or emotionally troubled. It is never too late to do this healing to create spiritual harmony. Even if your children are already grown but you suspect that they have been affected by this spiritual imbalance, you may do this healing for them.

People ask all the time if baby ghosts exist, and this is the closest thing that I have encountered. The baby does not haunt a location and does not even appear as a physical baby would. It is more a mass of dark, unhealed energy that hovers around the parents until it can be born into a new body or healed through love.

This healing may also be used for anyone who suffers from feeling unwanted or unloved by their mother. People often say that there is no love greater than a mother's love, and perhaps this is because of the energetic connection created while the baby is inside the mother's womb. In a sense, your mother's body created and housed you as a fetus. To feel unwanted or unloved by your mother may actually feel as if you are unloved and unwanted by your Creator. The wounds we inherit from our fathers are different and are not included here. However, this healing may help heal any imbalances that affected you as you were developing as a fetus. Many people simply did not get the love they needed from their mothers, and this healing restores the imbalance.

Healing an Unwanted Baby

You may do this healing on yourself and your children without their permission. If you do this for anyone else, you must get verbal consent. This healing is achieved through connecting with the Creator in the theta brain wave. Once you connect to the light at the highest level mentally, say:

Creator, it is commanded to send unconditional love to this baby, to restore any imbalances that were created and to heal all wounds with all involved in the highest and best way now. Thank you.

When you witness this healing, you will need to visualize a healthy physical baby inside the mother's womb. You may see dark energy leaving both the baby and the womb. This can happen very quickly or it may take a while. Just be patient and watch as the dark energy is replaced by light. Next, witness the Creator's unconditional love fill the mother's womb and every cell of the fetus until it shines brightly. You will know when this healing is done because you will feel it. At times I have seen the baby turn its head and smile at me. Even though this is a fairly simple healing, it is profoundly powerful and will make an immediate difference for both the living and the dead.

Animal Ghosts

Believe it or not, animal ghosts are fairly common. My only thought on this is that they may have stayed behind with their owner if they passed first. Animal companions can be incredibly faithful to the people who care for them that their bond extends long after death. If you experience a ghost animal, check around to see if their owner is a ghost still residing here. I don't believe that animal ghosts need to be crossed over. I believe that they will cross over automatically when their owner does. Most of what we experience in terms of animal apparitions are actually spirit animals that are just checking in on us but are not stuck.

TIGER

When we moved into our old Victorian home and began renovating it, we experienced a ghost cat for the first time. We actually had a cat, so our first response when we saw it was that the ghost cat must be our own cat. It was late at night and my husband and I were sleeping. Something woke me up and I noticed a cat beside my bed. Thinking that it was our cat, I reached down to pet him and he walked away from me as I watched him disappear into the wall. I sat up and looked around. Had my eyes played a trick on me? Our cat was not even in the room. The next time it happened, my husband saw the cat sitting on the floor beside his side of the bed. He reached down to pet him and his hand passed right through the cat as it disappeared.

Two weeks later, I awoke to find the cat sitting on the bed, right beside my pillow. It was clear that this was not our cat! His body was quite muscular for a cat and he appeared to be mostly black. Our cat was an orange tabby with a smaller build than the one I had seen. He sat there proud as he looked at me. Since he was just a foot away from my face, I could see him well. I blinked a few times to make sure my eyes were seeing what I thought they were, and his image remained, just as boldly as a living cat would appear. He licked his lips as he looked down at me, like he had just finished cleaning himself. Somehow I knew that it was a male cat and that his name was Tiger. I actually thought that was a funny name because I didn't notice any obvious stripes. The image of the cat lingered for longer than any other apparition I had seen in the past. I continued to look at him in awe, grateful that he hadn't disappeared from my sight. Then finally, his image began to slowly pixelate and he disappeared into thin air.

For some reason, Tiger wanted to make his presence known to us and seemed quite smart about how to get our attention. Perhaps he just wanted to be acknowledged, or maybe he needed to check out the new inhabitants of his home. Prior to that, we had noticed a cat smell at odd times, and before we could treat the area for odor, the smell would vanish. We often wondered if the previous owners had a cat, but we never assumed that it was a ghost cat sending us little signs of his presence.

We have noticed our cat staring into thin air and then quickly taking chase after something that we cannot see. Perhaps he is aware of the ghost cat and has accepted him as an invisible friend. Shortly after our experience, we felt compelled to adopt a black kitten that needed a home. Perhaps Tiger imparted that idea to us when he effectively communicated his name to me telepathically. We usually experience hints of Tiger in the lower level of our home, but we have also seen him roaming on the main level. The quick flash of his shadowy body running across our path has caused my husband to trip on more than one occasion. When he turns to look, both of our "real" cats are usually doing something like lying on the sofa in the other room. Sometimes we can also see Tiger out of the corner of our eyes.

Many people experience their pets in spirit after they have passed. It is actually quite common for beloved pets to stay around and continue loving their family from the spirit world. In the case of Tiger, he was not our pet in this life, but we have taken him into our hearts and family. When people ask how many cats we have, we say three: one orange tabby, one black kitten, and one ghost cat name Tiger.

Near-Death Awareness

Many people with a terminal illness experience having what is now called NDA (near-death awareness). Many of you are already aware of the NDE (near-death experience), in which a person comes close to death, experiences the other side, and then comes back. The NDA is different because the person is preparing for the transition of leaving their body for good.

Many people nearing death see the spirits of their loved ones. They may look off into the distance or seem to stare at a wall for no particular reason. The living cannot usually see the spirit world, and therefore we may assume that our loved one is losing their mind. However, what they are seeing is real and this is a completely natural part of dying. Often, they talk about having to go somewhere and feel that they are going on a trip of some kind. If you allow them to tell you what they see, they will be able to share this sacred time with you. They may tell you about certain loved ones in spirit who have come for them, or they may be surrounded by all their ancestors in spirit even if they never knew them in life.

Every person's experience with passing is different. Don't assume that your loved one is delusional because they say odd things or seem to ramble. Although they may seem incoherent, there is a lot going on for them. Part of them is focusing on the next phase of life while the other parts of them are starting to let go. It is best to just sit with them and offer love and support as they go through this process.

Many people wait for a certain occasion to occur before they finally let go. It may be the arrival of a grandchild, the marriage of a son or daughter, or a visit from someone coming from out of state. I have come to believe that we choose when we die and that there is somewhat of an order to our departure, even when death seems to be untimely or tragic. We have many doorways of opportunity to cross over, and our soul has a choice about which one we decide to take.

Volunteering for hospice has allowed me to work with people who are experiencing near-death awareness first-hand. Sometimes I am able to see the loved ones in spirit waiting bedside for my client to pass. I use my ability to communicate with the spirit world to do a spiritual analysis for my client. Sometimes I find that they have things to work out before they pass. Other times they just don't know how to let go of living.

When a person reaches this stage of life, they often spend time outside of their body as a spirit. They may travel to visit loved ones and then return to their body without anyone knowing. A living spirit can appear as an apparition before death. With the skills you've learned in this book, you will be able to communicate with them on both sides of life.

Environmental Causes for Hauntings
Carbon Monoxide

A carbon monoxide leak in a home or building can be the cause of an apparent haunting. Symptoms of carbon monoxide poisoning include headache, dizziness, nausea, flu-like symptoms, fatigue, depression, shortness of breath, confusion, and hallucinations. Many people look to carbon monoxide to explain away their ghostly sightings as perceived hallucinations. Many of the symptoms of carbon monoxide poisoning are similar to what a ghostly presence can feel like. Carbon monoxide is very dangerous and should be checked if you suspect that this may be the cause. If so, it will need to be repaired immediately! If you are a paranormal investigator, it doesn't hurt to add a carbon monoxide detector to your investigation kit. Carbon monoxide is a colorless, odorless, and tasteless gas that is known as the "silent killer." It is quite common for people to have a carbon monoxide leak and not be aware of it until it causes sickness or even death.

It is an excellent idea to check the home for possible carbon monoxide leaks if you even suspect that this could be possible. However, if you rule out carbon monoxide poisoning, you may have to face the fact that you do have a ghost. In the off chance that you actually have a carbon monoxide leak, it doesn't completely rule out that you may also have a ghost as well. Carbon monoxide poisoning is so deadly that it could solicit help from the spirit world to warn you, especially if you have protective spirits or ghosts in your home.

Here are some possible sources of carbon monoxide poisoning:

- Gas water heaters
- Kerosene space heaters
- Propane heaters
- Propane stoves
- Charcoal grills
- Gasoline and diesel generators
- Cigarette smoke
- Boats (any boat with an engine)

- Spray paint, solvents, degreasers, and paint removers
- Riding in the back of an enclosed pickup truck

Electromagnetic Frequencies (EMFs)

If your residence has a high EMF reading, it could indicate the presence of ghosts. When a ghost manifests, it can create a spike on an EMF meter, which indicates that a ghost gives off an EMF. Some homes seem to have consistently high EMF readings with or without knowledge of a ghostly presence. Ghosts actually need energy to communicate with the living, so a high EMF environment would appeal to a low-energy ghost. The high EMF can actually charge the energy of the ghost, making it is easier to communicate. High EMF locations tend to have a lot of unexplained supernatural activity. It is not quite clear which comes first, the chicken or the egg, but ghosts and high EMFs seem to go together.

Typically, a high EMF reading will be found around electronic devices, cell phones, Wi-Fi, and wiring in the home. However, if your home has a naturally high EMF reading, you will want to remedy the situation for long-term health benefits. While high EMFs help us to communicate with the dead, long-term exposure can cause many health problems in the living. Some of the effects associated with high EMF readings in the home include brain tumors, leukemia, birth defects, miscarriages, chronic fatigue, headaches, cataracts, heart problems, stress, nausea, chest pain, forgetfulness, and cancer.

Created Hauntings

Tulpa

A tulpa is a thoughtform of mental energy. The word is taken from Tibetan mysticism and is an entity created entirely within one's mind. A tulpa is something that is not talked about very often in the paranormal field. What it suggests is that a place may be haunted simply by the belief that it is. A paranormal investigator will not necessarily know the difference, because the evidence will be the same as with any other haunted location, the difference being that the agent of the haunting is not a deceased person but a belief in a ghostly presence. Don't get me wrong—a tulpa is real. If enough people believe in a ghost at a certain location, their thoughts will actually create one. In this case, there is no soul to heal or cross over, and the energy will need to dissipate in order to be cleared.

The field of quantum physics may help explain this phenomenon better. Scientists are now discovering that our thoughts carry real substance and that our thoughts alone can make physical changes in our body and environment. The power of belief can be responsible for people affected by generational curses and can also explain miraculous healings. A tulpa haunting will be cleared when the people who believe in it have changed their minds and have stopped believing in it.

If you suspect that you may be affected by this type of haunting, pull your energy away from it. Discontinue talking about it, and ignore the things that you feel are connected to it. A clearing with sage would be helpful as well (see chapter 13). Once you have done a clearing on the location, tell everyone who knows about the haunting that it has been healed. That way, their collective thoughts about the haunting can be released as well.

Poltergeists

If there is a teenager in the house, it is possible to have poltergeist energy that can be confused with a haunting. Sometimes when a person suffers emotional stress or tension, it can create poltergeist activity. This phenomenon is usually associated with teens or preteens who are entering puberty and may have some natural psychic abilities.

In *Harper's Encyclopedia of Mystical and Paranormal Experience,* author Rosemary Ellen Guiley describes a poltergeist as

> a spirit, usually mischievous and occasionally malevolent, which manifests its presence by making noises, moving objects, and assaulting people and animals. The term "poltergeist" comes from the German *poltern,* "to knock," and *geist,* "spirit." Some cases of poltergeists remain unexplained and may involve actual spirits. In other cases the phenomena may be produced by subconscious psychokinesis (PK) on the part of an individual.

If the investigation indicates that there are no entities present, then you will need to talk to the family about the possibility of a poltergeist. If the stress from a child or teenager is causing this to take place, it is a good idea to recommend counseling or seek an alternative healer to work with. Many adolescents don't know healthy ways to work off stress, and it is a good thing to learn before it causes harm emotionally and physically. Sports or anything active can help the body release the pent-up stress, and hobbies are a good way to channel excess energy. This is a situation that the family can work on healing together. Make sure that the teenager feels safe talking to grownups and/or parents about things going on in their lives. It may even help for them to take classes on or learn about supernatural subjects so they don't feel out of place. Finding out how to harness their own energy is very empowering and can help them in many ways as they grow into adulthood.

8: haunted and blessed land

There are areas around the world that are known to have increased supernatural activity. Some of these areas have vortex energy and other anomalies that affect the natural laws. Many of these locations attribute their unexplained happenings to higher-than-average levels of certain minerals in the earth that produce high magnetic levels. Other areas of haunted land seem to hold the trauma of a war tragedy in the very soil. Sometimes land has been cursed by someone in the past and the effects are still felt today. Then there are miraculous places around the world that millions of people travel to for healing. In this chapter, we will explore some of those areas and the reasons behind their amazing power.

Vortex

A vortex is a spinning energy that comes from within the earth and can be detected by the human body. There are many bioelectric energy points spread across the planet that most animals avoid. When ancient people hunted, they noticed that animals often avoided these areas and actually ran around them instead of through them. It is no surprise that the humans followed suit and began to avoid these strange energetic areas, too. It is said that horses and cats are most sensitive to vortex energy, although you will rarely see birds perched on trees within a vortex.

It is believed that vortices are junctions of ley lines or meridians that cover the earth's surface. Some vortices are dormant, while others are awake or are in the process of awakening. One unexplained phenomenon that seems to occur at all vortices is reports of disappearances. Some vortices have a higher disappearance rate than others. They all have high magnetic readings, and some people believe that they are doorways into other dimensions.

If you seek to find a vortex, you may not have to travel far. While there are some very powerful vortices that are well known, there are many undiscovered vortices found in nature around you. All you will need is a pair of dowsing rods or a heightened awareness of your body. There may also be clues pointing you to vortices that may be found in trees that grow with a twisted trunk or in whirlpools that spin in water. In terms of vortex energy, try not to think of it as positive or negative. You will be able to discern the difference by the way it makes you feel. However, the same vortex that you resonate with may be upsetting for someone else to enter. We all resonate with different energies.

If you are using dowsing rods to find a vortex, simply walk with them pointed straight ahead of you and follow their direction until they cross. Using your body to find a vortex is a bit different, because you will allow the energy to be felt within your body, as if you were the instrument. Sometimes when you enter a vortex, you will feel an expansive and warm energy in your heart. Other times you will feel a sickly feeling in your gut, or your head will spin. Vortices are very powerful areas in which to pray or meditate when you find one that resonates with you personally.

Your own home may have a natural vortex area within it. The energy from the land will permeate through the house and create areas that feel more comfortable than others as well as areas that people tend to avoid. If you have a cat, watch the areas in which they like to lie. Cats are very sensitive to energy and will often choose to lie in a favorable vortex area in the home. Finding a vortex in your home has some advantages. You can work with the existing energy and grow it with prayer and healing work to make it even more effective. I do a lot of healing in my office, and it has become the favorite lounging area for both my cats! When you meditate in a vortex, you will experience increased concentration, a higher vibration, clearer spiritual vision, and a more peaceful feeling. Vortices may also be created in any area through the power of intention and healing energy.

Bermuda Triangle

The Bermuda Triangle, also referred to as the Devil's Triangle, is one of the most famous vortices. It is located in the northwestern Atlantic Ocean between Miami, Florida; San Juan, Puerto Rico; and the island of Bermuda. There have been countless incidents of aircraft and surface vessels alleged to have mysteriously disappeared. One of the most famous disappearances in this vortex is known as Flight 19. In 1945, five Avenger bombers with thirteen crewmen from the United States Navy went missing after becoming confused and disoriented. Their planes were never recovered. Two mariners, or flying boats, were sent to rescue the distressed planes, but one of them never returned.

People have attributed these disappearances to the supernatural or paranormal. Some people believe that a doorway exists in this area that leads to another dimension. There appears to be a disturbance of natural laws that is often blamed for the unexplained occurrences and compass failure. Theorists ponder the connection to UFOs, alien interference, time travel, or a possible wormhole (which is a gap in space and time). There have been no conclusive findings about the anomalies experienced here, and this area remains a mystery.

Alaska Triangle

The Alaska Triangle, also referred to as the Devil's Graveyard, has a disappearance rate sixteen times higher than the national average. It is located between Anchorage, Juneau, and Barrows. The most well-known disappearance occurred in 1972, when two members of the United States Congress and two other men went missing. They were flying a Cessna 310 from Anchorage to Juneau and were never seen again. A massive search and rescue mission ensued for thirty-nine days before it was finally called off.

Supernatural activity remains high in this area, and scientists are incapable of explaining why. There are magnetic anomalies that cause navigation instruments to fail and could account for people getting disoriented and lost. However, that does not account for the fact that they never return. Like the Bermuda Triangle, the Alaska Triangle is a powerful vortex that may be responsible for the disappearance of planes, ships, and people.

Dragon's Triangle

The Dragon's Triangle, also known as the Devil's Sea, is located in the Philippine Sea south of Tokyo. This area is similar to the Bermuda and Alaska Triangles and is known for vanishing ships and seamen, and magnetic anomalies that still mystify scientists. The reasons behind such disappearances are sometimes blamed on UFOs and underwater civilizations.

Oregon Vortex

The Oregon Vortex in Gold Hill, Oregon, is an area known for the phenomenon of perceptual distortion. Many tourists flock there to witness the optical illusion effect of physical things and people shrinking and growing. This evidence can be captured in a photograph, so you can not only experience it personally but document it as well. The Native Americans called the area "Forbidden Ground," and it is said that their horses would not enter this vortex area.

Montana Vortex

The Montana Vortex, located outside of Columbia Falls, Montana, is a popular tourist attraction that allows you to watch your friends shrink and grow in the anomalous area of the vortex. There is also an area where you can stand and actually see the aura around your entire body! All living things emit an electromagnetic field, but most people are unable to see it. The Montana Vortex employs tour guides that can help you understand some of the paranormal effects that happen there.

Burlington Vortex

The Burlington Vortex in Burlington, Wisconsin, is said to induce experiences of spirit activity, seeing fairy kingdoms, and feeling the energy shift of other dimensions. I have actually experienced this vortex and have had amazing personal experiences. There is a different feeling in the woods, and the energy shifts with you as you move into different areas. At one point, I felt dizzy and disoriented as I walked up the side of a hill and realized that I had walked through a smaller vortex. When pictures were taken in that location, the images all seemed to be spinning. On a second visit, I took the guided tour and learned even more about this energetic power spot. This vortex is well worth a night visit to photograph the abundant anomalies. You will be able to capture dimension shifts, orbs, spinning portals, lights in the sky, and swirling doorways to other dimensions, and you may even experience levitation or partial invisibility. It was also clear as we walked the tree-lined path that no little critters inhabited those woods. We didn't see one squirrel or bird while we were in the vortex area. It was an odd experience to have absolute quiet in what would otherwise be restless woods. You will experience many things there that will leave you wanting to know more!

Sedona Vortices

The Sedona Vortices, located in and around Sedona, Arizona, are believed to have spiritual benefits that will help visitors to gain clarity in their lives. The energy seems to facilitate prayer, meditation, and healing. The subtle energy centers must be personally experienced, but it is claimed that they enhance spiritual and psychic powers. I have been to Sedona and have experienced feeling weightless while running up a mountain toward a well-known vortex. I felt clear-minded during my entire visit and experienced walking through an interdimensional portal. The experience was profound for me, and I have never forgotten it.

Great Serpent Mound

The Great Serpent Mound in Adams County, Ohio, is the largest effigy mound in the world. It was constructed as a large serpent with supernatural appearance and power. Over the years, the Great Serpent Mound has gained a reputation as a mystery spot where anomalous things happen quite regularly. It is said to be visited by ghosts of the dead mound builders. Many people report that it is spiritually centering and that their chakras became open by visiting the site.

Asheville Vortex

The Asheville Vortex is located in the Great Smoky Mountains in North Carolina. There are reported to be twenty-four active vortices between Black Mountain and Waynesville, as well as areas that are referred to as power spots. Asheville has one of the most concentrated number of vortices and power points anywhere in this country. I have stayed in the mountains near Asheville and experienced many feelings associated with vortex energy and high-vibration locations. This area has been calling out to holistic healers and metaphysical people who literally feel led to move there. This is a beautiful area in which to explore anomalous energy!

It is highly probable that you will experience mind-blowing changes to your current reality if you explore vortex sites and other supernatural locations. Strange and unexplainable anomalies occur in these areas, leaving the minds of scientists guessing at the causes. With such ample energy available, you are certain to experience paranormal events at these locations. Expect any devices you carry along to go bonkers!

Caves

Caves are dark, damp, and scary places to roam and make the perfect backdrop for any haunted story. However, caves actually do have all the right combined elements to create a haunting. The darkness experienced in caves creates sensory deprivation, which has been known to increase psychic awareness. Many ancients retreated to live in pitch-black caves in order to receive wisdom through their visions. The ancient Greeks sought enlightenment and altered states of consciousness by entering caves and staring into pools of water. Miners who were trapped in caves frequently reported hallucinations and visions.

Research by psychologist Wolfgang Metzger suggests that there is a conclusive reason for heightened ghostly activity in darkened locations. It has been found that when there is an absence of visual stimuli, the brain becomes more receptive to the total field. The total field is more than what we can normally see (for example, other frequencies such as the spirit world). Sensory deprivation allows us to be more receptive to seeing things that we normally would not be able to see. An experiment demonstrating the Ganzfeld Effect can help you to understand this phenomenon. It can be duplicated in your home by taping ping-pong-ball halves over your eyes, listening to white noise through headphones, and staring into a red light.

Dampness is a condition often associated with hauntings. It is said that water serves as a conduit between the spirit world and our own. Caves tend to maintain a high level of humidity, and some even house their own springs, waterfalls, and pools.

In many earlier civilizations, people lived as cave dwellers, which could account for some hauntings, too. Just as ghosts return to the homes they once lived in, cave dwellers may return to their caves after death. I also believe that the energy of the cave serves to hold the energy in place. This type of environment could be a catalyst for ghostly phenomena.

Wabasha Street Caves

The Wabasha Street Caves in Saint Paul, Minnesota, have long been considered haunted. The sandstone caves were actually manmade mines and were carved out of sandstone in the 1840s. It was once the home of the Wabasha Street Speakeasy and was a gathering place for gangsters, including John Dillinger. There have been many sightings of ghosts that look like gangsters from the 1920s. Paranormal groups have recorded many EVPs and experienced ample ghostly stirrings and documented encounters.

Ruby Falls

Ruby Falls is located within Lookout Mountain, near Rock City and Chattanooga, Tennessee, and derives its name from the wife of the man who discovered it. The Native Americans once used the limestone caves in Chattanooga, Tennessee, for shelter and to outrun their enemies. Civil War soldiers were brought there, as the cave was used as a field hospital, and notorious outlaws were said to have used this cave as a hideout. This cave is home to a natural underground waterfall that cascades an amazing 145 feet, which seems quite anomalous. They aren't sure where the water actually comes from that feeds the waterfall, as failed attempts have been made to discover the source. When touring this cave, I felt a strong connection to Native American spirits that still seem to be very present there.

Mammoth Cave

Mammoth Cave, in central Kentucky, is the world's longest-known cave system. Experts say that Mammoth Cave was in existence more than twelve thousand years ago. The extensive history of the cave began with visits from the earliest settlers. During the War of 1812, between the United States and the British Empire, slaves mined the saltpeter from the cave to make gunpowder. Shawnee and Cherokee Indians hunted the area and are said to have used the cave for shelter. Mammoth Cave was also used as a burial place by early explorers and cave dwellers. Over the many years of exploration, mummies have been discovered in the cave, which seem to have been preserved by the mineral content within the cave. There are many stories of haunted sightings and full-bodied apparitions in the cave. Tourists have reported seeing people dressed like early settlers who joined the guided tour and then disappeared.

Lemp Mansion Cave

The Lemp mansion in St. Louis, Missouri, is known as one of the most haunted houses in the country. Although the Lemp family was wealthy, their money could not relieve the massive losses they endured. Johann Adam Lemp emigrated from Germany in 1838 and settled in St. Louis, where he started a brewery. After his death, the family brewery was left to his son William, who expanded it and turned it into a national distributor of Lemp beer. William went on to groom his favorite son, Frederick, to run the family business, but Frederick, who was never in good health, was said to have worked himself to death and died of heart failure. William never really recovered from his son's death and withdrew from the outside world. He is said to have used the cave system beneath the house to reach the brewery daily. No longer able to function, William shot himself and died in his mansion.

William's daughter Elsa was having marital problems, and shortly after his death, she shot and killed herself in her St. Louis home. The next heir in line was William's son William Jr., who used the caves to store beer. He also built a ballroom, swimming pool, and theater in the caves. After losing the family money, William Jr. shot himself and died in his office inside the family mansion. Years later, William's other son, Charles, committed suicide by shooting himself and dying in the mansion.

After Prohibition, the cave was sealed shut and the house was used as a boarding house. This property would be an interesting investigation because of the family history and the cave system underneath the house. What led to so much tragedy? While the caves are probably not accessible, they may still contribute to the hauntings reported. The Lemp Mansion is now run as a restaurant and inn and is reputed to be one of America's most haunted buildings.

Tip: If your town was built upon an underground cave or tunnel system, it is highly likely that there is trapped spiritual energy there. Tunnels were used for anything from the Underground Railroad to alcohol smuggling during Prohibition. Both scenarios involved heightened human emotions and death, making them advantageous to investigate.

Sacred Grounds and Burial Grounds

Ancient civilizations often named things with the Devil's name when they knew that the area had supernatural powers but did not understand why. The ancients could not explain why these areas disobeyed the laws of physics, so they labeled them as having evil powers. In truth, most of them are affected by very natural elements that we understand better today. Crystals, minerals, magnets, underground caves, running water, and vortices all create conditions that set the stage for unexplainable supernatural events.

Devil's Tower

Devil's Tower, located in northeastern Wyoming, is among the most recognizable natural formations in the world. It is said to be one of the most powerful supernatural sites on this continent. Devil's Tower is a 1,280-foot rock formation with a flat top, and stands out from its otherwise flat surroundings. The Native Americans found that Devil's Tower was an excellent place for embarking on vision quests and used the sacred site for ceremonies of different kinds. They believed that the rock formation had supernatural powers and allowed them to have mystical insight. Devil's Tower is said to be haunted by Native American ghosts as well as many powerful animal spirits. It is no surprise to discover that there are very high electromagnetic readings there, which are said to induce religious experiences and higher levels of consciousness.

Burial Grounds

The Native American people lived very closely with Mother Earth and didn't need instruments to tell them how to find vortices. They paid attention to the animals that avoided certain areas and observed the anomalous growth of trees. It was common for them to hold sacred ceremonies in these high-powered areas. Most burial sites are located on a vortex. Many of the Native Americans believed that this energy would help them in the spirit world when they left their body. If you are respectful while visiting Native American burial grounds, you may encounter ghosts or spirits that stayed behind to protect the sacred site.

INDIAN WITH A BOWL CUT

While visiting a Calusa Indian burial site in Florida, I encountered a spirit that was not pleased with my presence. The sacred burial mounds had been turned into a state park to commemorate the Calusa Indians. It was my first time visiting the site, so I followed the trail to what they said was a ceremonial mound. There were two different-size mounds. The smaller mound sat at the base of a much larger one that had stairs leading up to the top for an overlook. I was nestled in under the tree of the smaller mound where they did their ceremonial dressing to prepare for sacred rituals. I brought an offering of tobacco and placed it in the earth and then closed my eyes to connect with the spirits. Immediately, there was a little dark-skinned man who was very angry. His face was right up to my own as he yelled and screamed at me in a language I had never heard. His hair was black and cut like someone had placed a bowl on his head and snipped around the edges. I remember thinking how strange it was, because my association with Indians had always included long hair and possibly braids. Though I didn't know what he was saying, it was clear that he did not want me on the area of land where I stood.

On my way out of the park, I noticed a trail marker with some history of the Calusa Indians that I had missed on my way in. When I stopped to read it, I was shocked to see the depiction of the Calusa Indians. The entire tribe wore their hair short in what is commonly referred to these days as a bowl cut. I couldn't believe it! My experience with the Indian spirit confirmed that I had indeed encountered a Calusa. It became clear to me that the Calusa Indian ghost was still protecting sacred land. The parks department didn't realize that the public trail was still thought of as a sacred location. In future visits, I left my tobacco at the base of the hill and stayed clear of the ceremonial area. The spirits were very pleased by this and welcomed our future visits.

Healing Waters

Fátima, Portugal

Millions of people travel around the world to sites that are considered to have holy water. In the early 1900s, the Virgin Mary appeared as an apparition to three children in Fátima, Portugal. The location was regarded as sacred, and the site became the destination for pilgrimages for people all over the world. The rural area did not have enough water for the pilgrims to drink or bathe in, and this caused some irritation among the local villagers. Finally, the decision was made to dig a new well for all the pilgrims to use. As the workers began to dig, they ran into a crusty rock layer that their tools could not penetrate. But mysteriously, the well began to fill with water. They never finished digging the well, but somehow it continued to produce water. Experts say that the closest access to water was over six miles away, and yet, to this day, "Our Lady's well" continues to flow in abundance. The villagers and pilgrims believe that the water there is miraculous. The faithful travel there to pray, while many people who are sick travel there to be healed. Countless miraculous healings have been experienced from drinking the well water.

Warm Mineral Springs

Warm Mineral Springs in North Port, Florida, produces nine million gallons of mineral-rich water per day. There are over fifty-one different minerals in the water, which ranks it as the third highest mineral content spring in the world. The water maintains a steady 87 degrees for comfortable year-round wading. The Spanish explorer Juan Ponce de León led an expedition to discover the mythical fountain of youth, which we know today as the Warm Mineral Springs. On his way to claim the spring, he was attacked by the Calusa Indians and died from the wound shortly after.

Visiting Warm Mineral Springs is a bit unsettling at first due to the smelly mineral sulfur. As you approach through a long corridor that houses showers and changing rooms, you will feel like you are entering a different time—like you have entered *Land of the Lost* and are about to experience a living dinosaur firsthand.

This site has actually become one of the most important underwater archaeological sites in the United States and the focus of underwater archaeology investigations. Scientists have discovered prehistoric human remains, saber-toothed tigers, giant sloths, and even a camel there. Wading in the springs is effortless because the high mineral content makes the water buoyant and easy to float in. My favorite experience at the springs is not knowing whom you will meet or what kind of stories they will share. Everyone has a healing testimony, which is what produces yearly visits from foreign travelers. Warm Mineral Springs is a true anomaly and should be experienced firsthand.

Cursed Land

It is possible to encounter land that is cursed. This type of land will seem to draw one tragedy after another to it. It doesn't matter where the land is or whether or not a house or building exists on it. Some people believe that such areas are the sites of a vile vortex, which is an energy vortex that doesn't resonate in healthy ways with people and other living things.

Many paranormal investigators are familiar with the infamous Villisca House Murders, which occurred in Villisca, Iowa, in 1910. This was the site of a vicious rampage that took the lives of an entire family, including children and two girls who were spending the night. The crime was never solved. The house is operated as a live haunted attraction that paranormal enthusiasts can pay to explore, investigate, and even spend the night in. It is interesting to note that some EVPs captured at the location indicate who the murderer was and coincide with the names of the suspects from that time.

In reading about the small town of Villisca, it is said that the name means "pleasant view." However, the history indicates that the name was changed and that the Iowan (Fox and Sioux) Indians actually called the town Willisca, which means "the place of devil spirits." Many people familiar with the story of these murders are not aware of the history of the land upon which the house sits.

The Villisca House was built on the site of a place where the Native Americans took their insane. Unlike the white men who built asylums to hide the mentally ill away, the Native Americans believed they would fare well in a different type of energy. Native Americans were closely connected with the earth and understood the nature of vortex energy. Many of their sacred sites and burial grounds are upon vortices. However, a vortex can affect the living in multiple ways. A vile vortex can make a person, animal, or plant unhealthy. However, if a person is already unhealthy, their energy would resonate in that energy field and they could be totally unaffected by the vortex. The Villisca House was built upon that site, and later the entire family met their demise. The house has never been a happy or healthy place for anyone who has tried to make it their home.

Why was that land in violation with nature to begin with? Could it be explained by the earth itself, the rock or mineral that lies beneath the surface? Could it simply be a vortex area that spins in the direction opposite to the direction that enhances most things in nature? If there is a supernatural anomaly in the land itself, it should be explored further to be better understood.

While experimenting with vortex energy, you will encounter some vortices that will make you feel healthy and balanced. Others will make you feel physically ill, and you will want to leave immediately. Many people believe those areas to be evil instead of understanding that they personally just don't resonate with that energy. Indeed, something is out of balance in a negative vortex area, but perhaps that can be healed instead of avoided or ignored. The same approach is helpful when encountering people as well. You will find that you will resonate with some and not with others. That is okay. It is actually natural law to go where you flow. Allow nature to lead you into perfect resonance with all those you allow into your life, the place where you work, and the home in which you live.

Curses Placed on Land

It is also possible that a parcel of land holds a curse that was put there on purpose. This type of curse was created and does not have to do with a vile vortex or any other natural anomaly. You may encounter a property that is haunted without having an actual ghost to blame it on. The land itself seems to hold a vendetta against wrongdoings of the past. These parcels of cursed land can cause continuous bad luck for home owners even hundreds of years after the curse was placed. Family members may fall ill, lose their jobs, and divorce at a higher-than-average rate. These areas are often home to violent supernatural occurrences that induce fear and unrest in the living.

Up until now, most people moved when they encountered a cursed house or parcel of land. However, just as the curse was placed on the land through intention, it may be removed through intention as well. Never, ever send a curse back to the sender, or to anyone else for that matter. Doing this will create terrible consequences for you in the future. It is always best to remove the curse and send it back to God.

Removing a Curse

A curse may be lifted and karma can be balanced through use of this simple healing technique. This is achieved through connecting with the Creator in the theta brain wave. Once you connect at the highest level mentally, say:

Creator, it is commanded to remove any curses from this land and send it into your light to be transformed into love and light. Thank you.

Witness the energy lifting off the piece of land and getting lighter as the darkness rises to the heavens. Then say:

Creator, it is commanded to heal this land and to fill it with Creator's love and to heal all people with energetic ties to this property, both living and dead. Thank you.

Witness the light filling the property, balancing nature, and inviting healthy species to inhabit the area. See the people in the area healing as well.

Trauma to Land

Civil War Ghosts

The most blood-stained land in the United States is no doubt that which was affected by the Civil War. While Gettysburg is well known for its ghosts, Chickamauga, Tennessee, is also known for hosting plenty of ghostly apparitions and disembodied voices from the massive casualties the war claimed. The Battle of Chickamauga (1863) lasted for two days and resulted in 35,000 deaths. Most Union soldiers were buried on the battlefield in mass graves. Not having a proper burial is often a catalyst for a haunting.

When the battle commenced, women searched through the injured and dead soldiers to find their loved ones. They searched into the night with lanterns but found little traces of life. Apparently, the agonized screams of women grieving their losses can still be heard on the battlefield, and the apparition of lanterns is still seen at night.

Oftentimes a spirit will not go into the light when they have suffered a cruel or untimely death. These young soldiers were not given a proper burial but instead were thrown into generic pits with multiple others. People are still discovering the bodies of Civil War soldiers. For many, the war is still happening.

Whenever there is such great tragedy and loss of human life, the tear-soaked land grieves. It holds the anguish and trauma from the human emotions that were poured into it. This actually creates a recording in the environment in the form of a scene that is played back over and over. The soldiers wander around aimlessly, and the land holds open the wound in need of relief. Both may be healed. It is time for our land to release this wound.

Land may be healed by doing prayer, meditation, and healing rituals. If you wish to pull the trauma from land, it should be treated just like a living being.

Healing Land

If land has been traumatized by war, battle, or murder, it can be healed. Everything holds energy to it, and this energy will be like an imprint of pain that scars the land. No matter what type of tragedy left its mark on a piece of land, it can be restored by doing a simple healing done in the theta brain wave.

How to Heal Land

1. Begin by sitting comfortably in a place where you will not be disturbed.

2. Close your eyes. Breathe in and out slowly to help you relax and get centered.

3. Feel the energy from Mother Earth come up through the bottoms of your feet.

4. Allow this energy to gently open each of your chakras as it rises to your crown.

5. Imagine that your consciousness goes out through your crown and above your space.

6. Continue moving your energy up until your eyelids begin to softly flutter.

7. State your intention to connect with God, Creator, or whatever your higher power is.

8. When you feel that your connection is strong, you may make this command:

   Creator, it is commanded to send any low-vibrating spirits or ghosts that are currently on this land into your light now. Remove any curses that were placed or tragedies that happened on this land, and heal all aspects of this land and anyone connected to it, both living and dead. Fill this land with vibrant healing light and restore its divine balance now. Thank you.

9. Imagine dropping your energy down from the Creator energy and into your home.

10. Envision the land in your mind's eye.

11. Witness the process. You will see dark energies move into the light. You may see visions of battlefields slowly dissolve. When the darkness has lifted, envision light filling every aspect of the land through all time. Watch nature respond with vibrancy to this change. When you feel the process is complete, it is. *Note: The process must be witnessed while connected to the light for it to work.*

9: ghost-busting devices

If you have been using the theta brain wave to connect to the light, you have probably already started communicating with spirits. If you are having trouble communicating or just want more validation, there are many tools that can help you. Thanks to the popularity of paranormal investigation television shows, the industry has created devices that can help you communicate with the other side more easily. The devices will offer you the ability to scientifically confirm what you feel, intuit, and see. There are many excellent websites where you can purchase equipment. My favorite online stores are Digital Dowsing (www.digitaldowsing.com) and The Ghost Hunter Store (www.theghosthunterstore.com).

Digital Recorder

Anyone interested in communicating with spirits should have a digital recorder for capturing EVPs. An EVP is speech (or speech-like sounds) heard on electronic devices but not heard in the environment at the time they are recorded. A voice you hear with your own ears is considered to be a disembodied voice, whereas an EVP is only detected on the recording. This may be because the EVP is a higher frequency that our ears cannot hear, like a dog whistle. All recorders have a different frequency range, so it pays to have several different ones on an investigation.

In the early days of my own investigating, I used a typical cassette tape to capture EVPs but did not have success with that type of recorder. Other people have used cassette recorders with success, but it is recommended to use a fresh cassette tape with each attempt at communication to ensure clarity. It is my preference to use a digital recorder for EVP sessions. Digital recorders can hold hours of recordings and automatically set up folders that help keep your investigations separated. They are easy to play back and are compact, and you won't run out of cassette tape! It is also easy to transfer your audio clips onto your computer to save or share.

I have a Sony digital recorder that I picked up at a local retail store for about $60. This recorder has a noise-canceling feature that makes the EVPs crystal clear—however, sometimes it can cancel out a quiet EVP. There have been times that I have captured an EVP on this recorder when others have not picked it up. Due to the clarity, I have used this recorder with a device called an EFP, which stands for EVP field processor. When I use the two devices at the same time, it allows me to watch the EFP for activation of lights, which indicates an EVP response. When the lights activate, I can listen to my recording for verification that communication with the spirit world has been established. An EFP device currently costs around $150 and can be purchased online. You will also need some good headphones when using this device. Headphones can be purchased from around $50 up to a few hundred dollars. You don't need top-of-the-line headphones—but you should have some that surround your ears.

The RT-EVP is a professional EVP instrument that is very much worth the investment. The device allows you to set an automatic playback while you are still recording. In other words, it allows you to get real-time answers to your questions during an EVP session. The recorder is very clear, and once you get the hang of it, you'll be amazed at what this little device can do! It also has a Spirit Box feature, which allows you to do frequency sweeps that the spirits can use to talk through. We have had great success using the frequency-sweep feature to have real-time conversations with the spirit world. The spirits are able to use the white noise that is created from the frequency sweep to communicate. Once you establish contact, it is possible to have multiple conversations. The combined features in this compact device make it a versatile tool to use on an investigation. The RT-EVP is currently available online for around $275.

The SB7 is a mini-size Spirit Box that made its debut on the *Ghost Adventures* "live" show from the Trans-Allegheny Lunatic Asylum on October 30, 2009. The Spirit Box is a frequency scanner that offers results similar to that of an

EVP recorder, but in real time. The frequency scanner is similar to the RT-EVP but is designed with only this one feature in mind. This model has an adjustable forward or reverse frequency-sweep technique coupled with a high-frequency white noise generator between frequency steps. This device is used for communicating directly with the spirit world and allows the spirits to use the frequency to speak to you in a way that you can hear them. This device currently costs about $80 and is well worth the investment.

THANK YOU FOR CROSSING ME

My daughter and I were using the SB7 Spirit Box and established communication with a helpful spirit one day. After clearly telling us his name, he told us where there were spirits who needed help. We went to the designated location and began to cross over the spirits who were trapped. In my mind's eye, I could see a stream of energy getting sucked up into the light while actually hearing the spirits talk through the Spirit Box. We heard many different voices saying, "Thank you," "Goodbye," "See you later," and "Thank you," and in a little girl's voice we heard, "Bye bye." It was amazing confirmation to hear the spirits communicate during their send-off to the other side.

If you're just starting out and don't have the funds for the devices mentioned so far, you will love this next one.

Let me set this up by saying that this is my little secret to consistently capturing EVPs. I had retired an old digital recorder to upgrade to the fancier ones as I became more active in investigating the paranormal.

During an investigation, all our batteries were drained in every device, and we realized that we were surrounded by ghosts. The only device that still worked was my old digital recorder. I stated that if the spirits needed to drain our batteries in order to communicate, it was okay. But they could at least say hello. Then we captured two *very* clear EVPs saying, "Hello," "Hello." So the old recorder was taken out of retirement and rejoined us on every investigation. It wasn't long before I noticed that the leader of the paranormal group that I belonged to used the very same recorder. Everyone had teased him because at any given investigation, he always captured EVP recordings when others didn't. They assumed that he was haunted or that his device was. However, I quickly validated that his cheap, older-model digital recorder was proving to be as effective as mine.

The recorder does not have a noise-canceling feature, so it sounds a little scratchy on playback. I believe what happens is that the recorder actually creates its own white noise—which makes it easier for spirits to communicate. You won't find this recorder on the retail shelves anymore. However, you can find it online. Everyone that I have told about this digital recorder has purchased one and had the same phenomenal results. They even sell these recorders in bulk, so it's not a bad idea to buy a bunch of them if you belong to a paranormal investigation group. Here is the make and model of what I think every paranormal investigator should have: Memorex Model MB2054. It should cost only $10 to $20.

I upload all my EVPs onto the computer to analyze. The Audacity software program works great for this and allows you to edit and save your clips. I've even saved some EVPs as a WAV or MP3 to upload to Facebook. If you don't already have Audacity, I recommend you get it. A free download is available at http://audacity.sourceforge.net. Now, these two nuggets alone were worth the price of this book. You're welcome, paranormal peeps!

EMF Meter

An EMF meter or detector is a scientific instrument for measuring electromagnetic fields. You will want to make sure you have at least one of these devices with you on an investigation. The EMF meter can detect ghosts and will indicate when they come close. I have the Mel Meter (Mel 8704R Vibe). The Vibe feature is a highly sensitive vibration accelerometer circuit that works as a touch sensor. If a ghost is nearby, you will be able to read the temperature (if there is a sudden cold spot), detect EMF fluctuations, and verify if an astral body is touching the device or trying to communicate. This device also has a backlit display, which makes it easy to read in the dark. It is currently available online for around $150.

The Mel 8704R MADD (Magnetic Anomaly Deviation Detector) also has some great features. The main difference between this Mel Meter and the Vibe is that this one has lights on top of the display that many paranormal investigators use as a means to communicate. You may have seen this feature used on ghost-hunting television shows: "Blink once for yes or twice for no." The light feature gives you yet another way to use this tool in the field. This device currently costs around $200.

It is well known within the paranormal industry that ghost activity happens in high EMF locations. It is very important to do baseline readings before an investigation starts so you know what the normal readings are for the location. Once the ghost communication starts and becomes more active, a spike will be indicated on the EMF meter. You could also add an EMF pump to the location to increase your chances of capturing evidence. An EMF pump acts like an actual pump to put more electromagnetic frequencies in the surrounding area. An EMF pump should cost around $90 to $200. You should not expose yourself to high EMFs for a prolonged amount of time, as it could be detrimental to your health.

ITC Device (Instrumental Trans-Communication Device)

The term instrumental trans-communication (ITC) coined by Ernst Senkowski in the 1970s and refers to communication between spirits or other discarnate entities and the living through any sort of electronic device, such as a tape recorder, fax machine, television set, or computer.

The Ovilus X is a talking ITC device designed for communication with the spirit world; however, the company claims that it is for entertainment purposes. We all know that there are no guarantees with any of the devices we use—and that they are all experimental. Collecting scientific evidence of the paranormal is a rapidly growing field. As the industry grows, the devices change and are upgraded. There is much to learn about the other side and how to bridge the gap in conversing with spirits.

I have an Ovilus X and have had some great results with it. I don't rely on the Ovilus X, but it has proved to be on target on many investigations. It has some great features, including a white noise generator and an EM pump. The only drawback to the Ovilus X is that you will need to get the digital screen display to be sure of the words it says. In an investigation setting, if you aren't sure if it said one thing or another, it will be difficult to communicate. Purchasing the digital screen display is a must to get optimal results with this device. The Ovilus X currently costs about $229, and the digital screen display costs an additional $89.

Spirit Photography

Believe it or not, I have captured a ton of anomalous images with a regular digital camera. It seems that it is pretty simple for spirits and ghosts to leave their mark on photographs. The strange thing about spirit photography is that sometimes an image can appear on the photograph at a much later date than the time at which it was taken. Hang on to your old photos!

When you are reviewing your photographs, you will want to make sure that your eyes are not what we call "matrixing." As humans, we try to find things we recognize, especially things with human attributes. As an infant, we learned pattern recognition. The recognition of patterns is a fundamental skill needed by animals to spot predators and is therefore associated with survival. Our mind still functions with pattern recognition even though we no longer live in the wild. Matrixing can also be considered "mind play," or seeing what is not really there. You will know the difference between matrixing and a real spirit photo if there were other anomalous happenings to suggest a spirit presence.

I have captured spirit photos with cheap throwaway cameras purchased at the checkout of any retail store, as well as digital cameras at all different price points. This leads me to believe that not only does the camera used have significance, but the photographer behind the lens does as well. Some people say that when you are ready to see spiritually, you will be able to photograph more evidence.

You will probably find that you resonate with a certain piece of equipment better than others. My digital camera was less than $200 and has been with me for a long time. I have captured spirit photos with it on a regular basis. My advice is to find a camera that works for you and stick with it.

Orbs

While some orbs are indeed dust and/or moisture, some are authentic spirit energy. To tell the difference, you will need to pay attention to other unexplained happenings. If you feel dizzy, tingly, or a heaviness and feel there is a spirit present, the orb in your photo may be authentic. If you capture an intelligent EVP and then photograph an orb, it may be authentic. I have taken a picture in the area of a ghost that I am communicating with and have captured an orb—even when no other orbs appeared in other pictures at the same location. Orbs are not clearly understood and continue to be investigated. It is possible for many different types of spirit energy to emerge from an orb, and you will need to rely on the way you feel in order to discern what they are.

Full-Spectrum Cameras

Ghosts exist in a vibration that the human eye usually cannot see. Humans see the range of light known as the visible light spectrum. The typical human eyeball can see the wavelength range of 380 to 750 nanometers. The various wavelengths in the spectrum of visible light are seen as different colors by the three types of photoreceptor cones in our central vision, spanning the full range of hues, peaking near the center of the visible spectrum at about 500 nanometers. That means that when we look at something, we do not see the frequencies that fall below 380 or above 750 nanometers. Those light frequencies are known as ultraviolet and infrared light. Paranormal investigators often capture ghostly images in the ultraviolet and infrared light frequencies. This means that spirits are always around us, but we are unable to see them because of our limited field of vision.

Our peripheral vision, however, allows in the ultraviolet and infrared light frequencies, which explains why so many people see things out of the corners of their eyes.

The peripheral vision is not used to distinguish colors, but is much better at detecting motion. This may be another reason people have reported seeing black shadow ghosts move from the corners of their eyes. The images they see are not actually black or shadowed—they only appear that way because their peripheral vision is unable to see color. Faint objects in the dark are better viewed by our peripheral vision. Our U.S. Army troops are often taught not to focus on objects directly at night but to direct their vision to one side in order to see them better.

Full-spectrum cameras should help us to detect the things that we cannot see with our eyes. I purchased a full-spectrum camera conversion but really haven't had much success with it. My advice here is to spend the extra money to get a really good-quality full-spectrum camera or piece of video equipment.

Night Vision DVR

I purchased the Sony Mini DVR-01 night vision, motion-activated camera. It detects passive infrared energy and motion fluctuations. Once I learned how to set up this camera for operation (it needs to be plugged into a TV or monitor to do this), I was pleased with the results. In order to work out the kinks, I set the mini DVR on a tripod at the end of our hallway. It is a great idea to get familiar with your equipment before using it in the field. I had set the night vision to snap three successive photos when the motion sensor detected something moving in the hallway. When I woke up the next day and retrieved the evidence, all I got was my husband's naked body walking back and forth like Bigfoot caught on film. Oops! Make sure you alert your family when you are trying out new equipment. In all fairness, the still photos were of great quality being that they were taken in pitch darkness.

I was very pleased with the overall functionality of this device. Whether you suspect there is an active location in your home or you use this device to monitor an investigation, I recommend it. Additional cameras can be added if you wish to monitor more than one area simultaneously. Sony Mini DVR currently costs around $170.

Pendulum

I used pendulums to detect properly functioning chakras and the subtle energy of the human body long before I knew they could be used to detect a spiritual presence. Just as radios pick up information from unseen radio waves, the pendulum is like a powerful antenna that receives information from the vibrations and energy waves emitted by people, places, thoughts, and things. It makes sense that a ghost—which is known to have a subtle energy body— would be detected by using such a device.

Albert Einstein was known to perform impressive feats with dowsing tools and believed that dowsing had to do with electromagnetism. Some people say that the pendulum creates a bridge between the logical and intuitive parts of the mind. Some say that the pendulum connects them with a higher power and call it "divining," as the information is believed to come from a divine source. Scientific research indicates that the pendulum responds to electromagnetic energy that radiates from everything on earth.

The pendulum has been used to detect allergies and other ailments and even to accurately determine the gender and birth date of unborn babies. It has been used to locate water, gold, oil, and other minerals. Many people use the pendulum to get answers to life's issues. In France, physicians have used the pendulum to assist them in making diagnoses. During the Vietnam War, U.S. Marines were taught to use a pendulum to locate underground mines and tunnels for survival. Whether we understand exactly how and why the pendulum works doesn't seem important compared to the fact that it works and always has. This instrument can also be an effective tool to use on paranormal investigations.

While holding the chain of the pendulum between your finger and thumb, it is customary to ask a question. Typically, the pendulum will swing forward and back to indicate "yes," and swing from side to side for a "no" answer. It may also swing in clockwise circles for "yes" and counterclockwise circles for "no." Not all pendulums work well with every person. If you want to use a pendulum for divining of any kind, it is important that you find one that works well for you. The more you work with and trust the results of your pendulum, the easier divining with it will become.

When you enter a "haunted" location, you will ask the pendulum to indicate the presence of ghosts on the property. You may also ask questions to determine the number of ghosts present by stating, "There are two ghosts here." The pendulum with tell you yes or no. If you get a positive response, then continue by stating, "There are three ghosts here," "There are four ghosts here," etc. You may be more direct and ask the pendulum if it is a male or female ghost and determine the age of it and how long it has been there.

Working with the pendulum may open up new doorways for you as you continue on your investigative journey in working with the spirit world. Once you have used the pendulum effectively, you will notice that your body also reacts to the environment and that this tool can help you to develop your own mediumship abilities.

Dowsing

It takes time to learn how to use dowsing rods properly and to develop a sort of relationship and trust with them. Dowsing rods can be made of anything and are usually shaped in the form of an "L." Many people bend wire hangers to use for dowsing. Forked twigs in the shape of a "Y" have also been used successfully for dowsing and were used before metal dowsing rods were created. Dowsing can even be done with the human body. Dowsing is as old as humankind and usually involves using the rods or sticks to help find things. With practice, everyone can use this technique.

Dowsing was considered the ancient art of *rhabdomancy*. As people seemed to lose their ability to use their intuition, they adapted by using tools to assist them. Dowsing has been around since written records have been kept. The ancient Egyptians and Babylonians dowsed using split reeds. The Chinese art of feng shui is said to have evolved from rhabdomancy. The Romans and Greeks used dowsing. Even the early Jews used dowsing for their own benefit. German dowsers successfully located veins of tin, which allowed mines to be established in the fifteenth century. But sadly, during the Middle Ages, dowsing became associated with the mystical unknown and the occult, and dowsers were accused of witchcraft and were killed.

Later, scientists established that somehow dowsing and electricity were linked. In England, dowsing was accepted as part of folk culture, like horse whispering, spellcasting, and stone divination. They were all considered to be of value, and people claimed that they were indeed effective. Therefore, dowsing was not dismissed as the work of the Devil and survived as it was handed down generationally. Many times, religions have made things seem evil when they simply didn't have a scientific explanation for how they worked.

Dowsing has been used to successfully find underground water, gold, minerals, oil, missing people, lost items, and even unmarked graves. It can also be used to read spiritual energy and overall health. Dowsing simply provides us with a tool to use to accurately follow our own intuition and innate guidance.

Using dowsing rods on an investigation will be similar to using a pendulum. Once you establish which way the rods will swing for "yes" and "no" answers, you may ask the questions you seek. An added benefit of using dowsing rods is that they can actually point you in the direction of a ghost. If they point to the left and parallel each other, then walk to the left. Keep following the direction of the rods until they crisscross—at which time, you should bring out the EMF meter or other device to confirm the presence of a ghost. When using dowsing rods, X marks the spot and will indicate the energetic field of the ghost or entity. Albert Einstein is said to have favored the use of dowsing and is quoted as saying:

> I know very well that many scientists consider dowsing as a type of superstition. According to my conviction this is, however, unjustified. The dowsing rod is a simple instrument which shows the reaction of the human nervous system to certain factors which are unknown to us at this time.

Ouija Board

While the Ouija board is not a device used on a paranormal investigation, it may appeal to those of you who wonder what is haunting your home. Most people in search of spirit communication leave no rock unturned, and many times this leads them to use the talking spirit board. There are many paranormal investigators who will blame a "haunting" on the client's use of the Ouija board without looking any further for a cause. In fact, if they see one in the home, that will usually be their immediate response.

It is my opinion that the Ouija board is no different than any other divination tool, including the pendulum, dowsing rods, or even the signals from your own body (such as tingling, goose bumps, or dizziness). Ouija boards are not evil in any way. In the spirit world, we tend to attract energies similar to our own—like attracts like. The effectiveness in using such a tool depends on the experience of the person using it. I do not believe that using the Ouija board opens doorways to the spirit world, because the spirit world exists all around us at all times independent of the board.

It is possible for a person to play with the Ouija board as a thrill-seeking device and attract an entity that is disruptive. It is just as likely that if a person set their intention, without the board, they would have the same result. People are plagued by bad spirits all the time. The spirit world is always waiting for us to pay attention to them or establish contact, and they will attempt to communicate whether or not we have a device of any kind. That being said, you would not invite communication with just anyone in the world of the living, and you should follow the same protocol when communicating with the spirit world. You are the boss, and it is you who sets the intention.

If you have any fear surrounding use of the board, don't use it. Fear is a powerful magnet that will draw unwanted energy to you. When using the Ouija board, it is a good idea to be respectful. I have always had good experiences using the board and go about it with the same reverence as when doing a healing or reading with the living. Light a candle and burn some incense to hold a higher vibration, and set your intent to communicate only with higher-vibrational spirits of loved ones or those in your highest and best. If you get used to connecting with spirits in this way, it could also help to prepare you for direct communication. After a while, using the board will seem like driving in the slow lane, and you will find that linking directly with a spirit is much faster.

Scrying

Some people scry into tea leaves to do future readings for people. Others scry into clouds or crystal balls. There are many ways to scry, but the technique I learned was from a wonderful medium and teacher and is designed to view the past lives of your sitter. Two people sit across from each other with a white candle lit on the table between them. Both people gaze into each other's eyes (or brow bone area) with the intention of seeing into other places and times. Allow your eyes to relax and go gently out of focus. If any of you read the book *The Celestine Prophecy*, you will recall that giving your attention to another person (or animal, plant, etc.) actually enhances their aura. If you are able to see auras, you will be able to see it illuminate and grow when attention or love is provided. We literally build or tear down others' energy fields all the time with our attention given or withheld. If that energy is returned through concentrated focus, the frequency around both subjects becomes very high. It has been my experience that doing this for any length of time (usually ten to twenty minutes) will cause the veil to drop so that you may see into the spirit world. It is very important to hold the energy as it grows by not talking or moving. You can blink as usual, but try not to startle when you begin to see past-life faces on your sitter. This is a fairly simple technique that everyone can do.

Many times, I have experienced spirits of loved ones that superimpose on or around the sitter while holding this focus. The more you practice scrying, the better your eyes get at "seeing" into the spirit world. This technique can be done anywhere and is easy enough to do on location as well. As always, surround yourself in the light so you only attract spirits and experiences that are in your highest and best and all others are shielded.

Flashlight

Let's not forget the basics here. Most of the time, hauntings are investigated at night. That doesn't mean that ghosts only come out to play at night, it just means that it is easier to photograph them then. Infrared or night vision cameras require darkness to work. Ghostly activity can happen at any time of day or night. Sometimes the ghosts will get rowdy and turn the lights off during an investigation. It always pays to be prepared and to have a flashlight handy. The pocket-size LED flashlights are very inexpensive and work great in the field. Everyone in my group carries one. I purchased mine from a paranormal supply store for about $15 and was shown up by my group members who had picked up theirs at a local retail store for only $4.

Equipment Bag

Whether you will need an equipment bag depends on how many electronic devices you are planning to use or bring with you. They make canvas-style overnight bags with many pockets, which work great for investigations. The more pockets the better, so you can keep your equipment separated yet easy to access. Most paranormal supply stores also sell hard-cover briefcases with foam padding that you cut out to fit each device you bring. This type of case is very sturdy and will protect your equipment in the field.

Batteries

I have to mention batteries here to make sure that they are not overlooked! It is well known that a ghost presence can drain your batteries. You should check all your batteries before you begin an investigation, but don't rely solely on that. I have experienced all my equipment being drained at exactly the same time, even though every device had new batteries. You don't want to get stuck at an active location with this problem, and it can be easily overcome by bringing *lots* of extra batteries!

Notebook and Pen

Bringing a notebook and pen to document activity is an exceptional idea. You will be able to record what type of results you get in different locations. It is a good idea to write down the time of any activity so that when you review evidence later, it is easier to find on a recording. Write down anything that you think could be important, such as temperature fluctuations, sounds, and feelings. For years I have kept what I call my paranormal journal. In it, I write down the date and time of all ghostly encounters I experience at home. Upon review, I have discovered that many of the dates correlate with the anniversary of loved ones who have passed. More often than not, the activity was just a spirit popping in to say hello and not a haunting at all.

10: investigating
your haunting

For those of you who are experiencing a ghost, the information in this book will help you resolve the haunting. Before we start, there are some questions that I need to ask, and your answers will help to determine what you are dealing with. Did anyone you know recently pass? Did the activity start around the time of the passing, or did it exist before? Have you recently moved or done any major renovations on your home? Have you purchased any used items from auctions or antique stores or been given any family heirlooms? Have you had a guest over recently who uses drugs? Has the content of your dreams changed dramatically? Have you been knocked unconscious or recently undergone surgery? Does the presence seem menacing or harmful in any way? Can you determine when the activity first began?

If you have lived in a home for years and then suddenly began to experience strange and unexplainable things, something has happened. You can be the best investigator for yourself because you know what things have gone on in your life and the lives of those around you. Being able to pinpoint the incident or starting point is often how you will determine what is causing your haunting. It could be that one of your family members unknowingly dragged something home with them. If someone you know died, it could just be their spirit trying to say goodbye to you. Or it could be that your recent renovations exposed some trapped energy in your home. I have known many people who have awakened after surgery and discovered that they could see things that they couldn't before. Sudden onset of spiritual vision can be alarming because it comes without instructions. This can make a person question everything they were taught, and it will test their beliefs on all levels.

If you moved into a new house and pretty much knew something was awry right from the start, chances are good that the activity has something to do with the property or house itself. If you're the owner, it will be easy for you to follow the paper trail of previous owners. You should be able to determine if there have been any deaths on the property. Natural as well as tragic and untimely deaths can contribute to a haunting. Remember, every person has free will when they die and can decide to go into the light or to stay behind.

Many people react with fear to a haunting and believe they have a demonic presence instead of a ghost. It is possible to encounter a ghost that just doesn't want anyone else living in their home, or they may not like females/males/

children/pets. It is possible for ghosts to be a bit menacing without actually being evil. Keep a check on the emotional status of your family to ensure that no one is feeding the ghost or entity through fear. Also, make sure that no one is being emotionally affected by the ghost. You'll notice if someone in your family suddenly becomes irrationally angry or lethargic.

If you are jotting down the odd things going on in some type of journal, you may notice that an apparition is seen at the same exact time or location in the home. It is helpful to know if the ghost is an imprint or an actual interactive and possibly troublesome guest. You may suspect which areas of the house are the most active, and it would be those that you should monitor. EVPs may be collected to help you discern what type of ghost is present and if they are capable of communicating. As with all spirit communication, be sure to say a prayer for protection before you engage the ghost (see chapter 13). Upon completion of the session, disconnect your energy and clear off with a closing prayer. This could be any prayer of your choosing or you could simply make one up. The purpose is to close the communication link and to disengage any energetic connection between you and the ghost.

If you are not interested in collecting evidence and just want the ghost gone, you can do that without knowing who it is or what they want. This is your home now, so don't feel that you have to investigate the haunting. Most people prefer to know how and why their house is haunted and by whom—to prove that they aren't crazy for seeing and experiencing the things they do. However, it is not necessary for you to investigate the haunting if you just want to cross it over (see chapter 5).

Setting Boundaries

If you have collected EVPs, they should not be played after the house has been cleared. This can actually reattract the entities, especially if the EVPs are played over and over or if there is a sort of emotional bond created through listening to them. It may be okay to listen to them at a much later date, but the best advice is to not ever play them again. If you want to show them to a friend, go away from the house to listen.

If you spend a great deal of time watching television shows about hauntings, reading books about ghosts, holding séances, or trying to communicate with spirits, chances are you will connect with some ghostly energy. Therefore, it is important to set up some boundaries beforehand. If you desire to help ghosts cross over but don't want the constant drama of having them around, tell them when they can come to you. Set a time of day when you will be available to help them so they don't infringe upon your daily life. After you have taken a few minutes to help them, move on with your day.

As a general rule, ghosts are not allowed in my bedroom. There was a time when they surrounded my bed at night, and they would be the first thing I would see upon waking, just standing there, waiting for me to help them. At times, they even attempted to enter my body.

Thankfully, I am so accustomed to doing the work I do within the spiritual dimensions that even in my sleep I evict entities and cross over troublesome ghosts. It's not much different than a waitress who still serves drinks in her dreams. However, all my work is done in the spiritual dimension, so it is normal to continue that work at night-time. My husband and daughter have both woken me up when they heard me making strange sounds in my sleep. Upon waking and recalling everything, I always double-check to make sure that all my work was accurate and complete. This has happened enough times that I just trust the process now.

It didn't take long before I set up some boundaries and decided not to allow any ghosts to enter my bedroom at all. It is simple to set up a boundary. Simply say in your head or aloud:

Ghosts and lower-vibrational entities must stay outside my home. I invite whom I want to visit, and you are not invited. My bedroom is off-limits. My body is off-limits. My home is off-limits. Thank you.

You are the boss and you get to set the rules. Oftentimes a haunting can be self-managed as soon as the homeowners realize that they have the power to do so.

11: paranormal groups

Now that you have the training and knowledge to get rid of a haunting, you may wonder if working with a paranormal group is right for you. Most paranormal investigators were once haunted, too. It seems that people drawn to work in the paranormal field are those who have experienced the spirit world firsthand. Some have lost a loved one and seek to understand what happens after death. Others have encountered a ghost, and some have actually lived in haunted houses. It is normal to have increased interest in the paranormal after experiencing things that cannot be explained. It is also very common for a person to triumph over a haunting and then seek to help others who are haunted.

Paranormal groups have taken off in recent years to the point that every state has many different groups to choose from. Not long ago, the subject of ghosts was taboo. Now, there are many paranormal groups available to assist the public in making sense of the invisible inhabitants that reside within their homes. These people are dedicated to working with the dead and oftentimes offer their services for free. Think about the long hours involved, the transportation costs, and the investment needed to purchase devices used in the field. There is no question that paranormal investigators are dedicated to the services they provide. If you are considering joining a group, it is important to find the right fit for you. There are basically three types of groups out there.

Some paranormal investigation groups are focused strictly on research and work to document evidence through scientific means as a way to prove the existence of ghosts. Their research often involves revisiting haunted locations over and over to gather as much verification as possible. For instance, they may note that there was an increase in unexplained activity when they used blue lights rather than green or red lights in a room. They will chart the weather, humidity levels, and moon phases of an investigation to detect patterns. They will look to see if a different combination of investigators triggers more active responses than others. Research groups help to move the industry forward with their impartial scientific approach.

There are paranormal groups that use different methods of communication that would be considered less scientific in terms of evidence. These groups consist of mediums and trained psychics who can intuitively read the environment to discover the cause of the haunting. Many paranormal groups that include mediums and psychics also use scientific instrumentation to document evidence. It would be common in this type of group to have the intuitive part of the team arrive at the location with no knowledge of it or the activity that has been experienced there. They would go through the property first to find the "hot spots" where a lot of activity occurs and alert their team about their impressions about the location. They may encounter a ghost or spirit who is willing to communicate with them and then document their conversation on paper. The intuitive is used as a sort of lead for the rest of the team and can make it more likely that the team will capture the evidence they seek based on knowing where to set up the cameras and how to approach the investigation. It's really exciting when the intuitive says what the ghost is communicating to them while simultaneously gathering the same information on the scientific gadgets via EVPs, Spirit Box, or Ovilus.

What has evolved from the previous group of investigators is a different type of paranormal group. The next natural step of investigating ghosts is healing the environment and releasing the trapped spirits who reside there. Yes, some groups specialize in crossing over ghosts. I have had the pleasure of working with all three types of paranormal groups but find myself being drawn to the latter. I work with spirits all the time in my daily life, and my healing abilities allow me to cross over spirits and work with healing on both sides of the veil. Because of my healing background, I could only hear EVPs saying "Can you help me?" so many times before needing to do something for them. I pray that more groups will decide to embark on this specialized portion of working with the spirit world, because it is only then that I feel we are truly helping those in need, both the living and the dead. Working from this perspective leads to a wider understanding of the spirit world, and it is impossible for it not to change the way you view life.

Helping the Haunted

When a family is experiencing a haunting, it is a very scary time for them. As a paranormal investigator, you will need to be sensitive to what they are going through. You will be entering the investigation with the experience to back up your knowledge, but the family may have none. Or even worse, they may only know what they have seen in movies, which could escalate their fear considerably. As a professional, you will need to address the family's needs and explain things to them in a way that they will understand. They may not understand paranormal jargon about your equipment or know much about the spirit world in general, so keep your summary short and simple. Whatever you do, make sure that you do not create more fear in a situation that is already charged. It is important to tell the truth, but do it in the highest and best way for your client.

Every time you experience something new in the paranormal field, you gain knowledge. With this knowledge comes wisdom. Don't expect to know everything on your first time out or beat yourself up for making a mistake early on. However, if you are a seasoned investigator, you should be accountable from start to finish on an investigation.

Let's address some misinformation that fuels the public fear of the unknown.

There is nothing worse than feeling like you need spiritual help and not being able to find any. This is just not the kind of thing you can ask your neighbor for! A family desperate for help will probably have already tried many things to get rid of the haunting before they contact a paranormal team. Most people these days go online and seek answers from a Google search. But who posts this stuff and what kind of background do they have? If you Google "how to cross over a ghost," you will find loads of misinformation, such as, "Tell it to go to the light." That apparently was not written by someone who can see into the spiritual dimension, because if they could, they would know that there is no light.

Without going into a full review of chapter 5, "Crossing Over Ghosts," it is worth mentioning again: a ghost does not have access to the light, which is why they are essentially trapped and hanging out where they don't belong. If a person experiencing a haunting reads that misinformation, they are likely to feel even more helpless after they try it and it fails. The activity may even escalate, and the vulnerable and scared individual may finally break down and call a priest. But the priest may or may not come to their aid. I have known several people who were really in need of spiritual protection and the church refused to help them because they were not a regular parishioner.

The good news is that with a little practice, anyone can clear a haunted house themselves. There were many reasons for me to write this book, one of which was to help people navigate the spirit world without fear. Once you know what you are dealing with and you understand the spiritual laws, there are no worries.

Mediums can be a very helpful addition to a paranormal team because they are the ones who will cross over the ghosts. This person will serve as your intuitive, and do the initial walk-through and the final crossing. I must admit, sometimes it is frustrating to watch television shows about people who work in my industry and spread misinformation about it. There was a medium on television who would scare innocent homeowners into selling their homes because she didn't know how to cross over ghosts and entities. There was another show where a guy would tell victims of a haunting that an item in their home was the cause. He would then take the item and add it to his own collection. Really! As we now know, it is simple and easy to clear a home, land, or inanimate object. I hope those shows were just shooting for high ratings and that the people involved don't actually work that way.

After the home has been cleared of any unwanted energy, it is important to talk to the family. You should have discovered the reason for the haunting, which is good information to share with the family.

Haunted by a Non-Familiar Ghost

If you have something in common with a ghost, sometimes they can form an attachment to you and follow you home. It makes them feel like they are still living, but, of course, it is not fair to you. If you are a painter, you may attract a fellow artist, or if you love to read, you may attract a writer.

There have been cases where a house was being haunted by someone who never lived there. These can be extremely random types of hauntings that may be difficult or impossible to research. You may need to trust your team intuitive and the evidence alone with this type of haunting.

GHOSTLY NEIGHBOR

One time, we encountered an old man ghost in a home that we were investigating. He had never lived in the home, but he did live and die next door. His family eventually moved out, and he roamed over to the neighbor's house and essentially set up home there. This is actually a pretty common phenomenon. If your historical research fails to turn up any leads for the haunting, broaden your search, starting with the surrounding areas in closest proximity and working out from there. When we gave our detailed description of the old man that we encountered, the home owners immediately knew who we were talking about. We did a healing for his spirit to raise his vibration and essentially cross him over. He still visits there as a spirit but cannot drain the living.

If the family unwittingly invited the ghost into their home, they will need to know not to do it again after the crossing. It could have been something as simple as a child wishing to have a ghost to play with. A person could also attract a ghost out of loneliness or the need for excitement or drama. Many people who watch ghost investigation shows fantasize about how cool it would be to have a ghost, and then they get one and don't know what to do with it. Other times ghosts appear for a random reason, which is why everyone should learn how to energetically protect their home and cross over ghosts.

Investigation Protocol

Many people head into an investigation without knowledge of how to conduct an investigation. They may have to sift through hours of contaminated EVPs because others in the group were talking. If several people compete for the same position, it can create confusion and ineffective results. Although each person in the group is of equal value, there should be one leader. This person should have the most experience in the field and can provide stability for the team during highly charged situations. It will save you time and effort if you get used to following a certain protocol while working with a paranormal investigation team.

Each investigation is like an adventure and will need to be planned out well. You should have one team member who focuses on finding locations to investigate. They will talk to the owners, get clearance from whoever is in charge, and arrange the investigation date. Most of the time, this person is not an intuitive. (The intuitive on your team should *not* have any prior knowledge of a haunting.) However, the scheduler is very important to the group's survival. This person functions within the group as a sort of liaison to the outside world and handles any media coverage that the team gets. It will be up to this person to navigate the group toward cases where they will be most beneficial to the clients and at the same time have the most fun. Let's face it, while this is important work, you will probably be doing it for free. You'd better enjoy this work and have fun, or it is time to hang up your gear and go home.

Doing historical research on the haunted property can take some time and commitment, so this can be assigned to a person on the team who knows their way around the library. Most of the information will be free to access. I have had success using microfilm at the public library, talking to town historians, and going to the courthouse to view tax records. The more information you have, the better prepared you will be when you enter the haunted location.

Before leaving for the investigation, someone should check the equipment bag and make sure that everything is packed. A device specialist can make sure that everything is in working order. The memory sticks for the digital cameras should be empty and ready to use, and all devices should be fully charged, with extra batteries packed.

Make sure that people outside your group know where you are going. In other words, for safety, keep track of the address and contact information for each investigation site that you go to. In case anything happens, supernatural or not, you will be easy to track down. Let's face it, most investigations are done at night, and sometimes you will find yourself in locations that don't have cell phone service.

The moment you arrive at the location, you should say your protection prayer as a group. It is a good idea to make this connection with your team members so you can ascertain any changes within them as the night goes on. If one of your members gets something attached to them, you will see the difference right away and be able to take care of it. In the field, you are more than each other's eyes and ears; you are each other's spiritual protectors.

It is not advised to have the family or client present during the investigation. If your scheduler did their job right, they have already talked to them and documented the activity going on. Now, it's time for you to do your job. Allow the intuitive in your group to walk the grounds and lead you through the building. Follow their advice about where they feel or sense paranormal activity. It will take quite a lot of trust for the team to follow the intuitive person's lead, but trust is fundamental to having a successful team anyway. You want to know that the people you are going into battle with can and will protect you. If there is one weak link, it can bring the whole group down. One of the team members should be noting what the intuitive gets and earmarking locations of apparent hot spots for the investigation.

It is okay to do the baseline EMF readings of the location while the intuitive is doing the walk-through. This should be a three-person job, with the intuitive picking up any psychic impressions from the location, the tech person getting baseline readings, and the note taker writing down anything pertinent that the other two say.

Once the walk-through is done, the team will be able to make a game plan of the night's investigation. If you brought motion-detection cameras or video-monitoring gear, this would be the time for the team's technical setup. Some groups actually set up a base station where they can monitor many computers at once while the rest of the team members investigate. If your group uses a base station, then now is the time to run power cords to all the areas that will be monitored. Make sure to tape the cords to the floor so that no one trips on them when it is dark. If you can, keep the cords tucked in the corner and not down the middle of the hallway!

If your team is not heavy into tech gear, don't worry about it. You will still know certain areas that the investigation will focus on, and you can prepare those areas by removing items that could be tripped on. You will want to know if windows and doors are open or closed, and if there are things that could confuse the investigation later, like a hamster living in the closet! Check for pets and electronic devices that make irregular noises so you will know that it is not a paranormal noise later in the evening.

If you do your investigation in the dark, then it is time for lights out! You may want to begin by conducting an EVP session in one of the hot spots. Introduce yourself to the ghosts and don't try to provoke them. Every ghost used to be someone's loved one. Treat the ghost as if it were your loved one who had passed. This approach will bring you more rewarding experiences with the spirit world. Be respectful and you are more likely to get really great communication and evidence rather than chaos and things being thrown. The ghosts use whatever energy they can in order to communicate. This means that they can use your energy, too. When an inexperienced team provokes through threats, insults, or yelling, the ghosts can utilize that energy to use it against you. Those are the types of investigations that get completely out of control and can put your fellow investigators in danger. We call this irresponsible investigating.

A short EVP blast session works well to see if you have a ghost present that is willing to communicate with you. A blast session means that you should only ask three questions timed about five to ten seconds apart. Listen to your recording to see if you have any feedback. Keep up the short EVP blast sessions in different locations until you establish contact. One of your investigators may want to take still photos at this time.

You may use trigger items if you know any information about the ghost. For instance, if it is believed that the ghost is a child, then use a toy or ball as a trigger item to link with them. If you leave a trigger item in a room being monitored, make sure you mark the floor where you set the item. That way, if the item moves, it will be on video and you will be able to verify how far it moved. A trigger item could be anything from the time period in which the person lived or a personal item that they were fond of. We have even used ourselves as trigger objects and dressed in period clothing to reenact a show in a haunted theater. If you use your imagination, your investigations can be very rewarding. But never do anything you feel uncomfortable with on an investigation.

When your team has finished investigating, it is time to pack up your gear. Please show the ghosts some respect and thank them for communicating. If you have someone on your team who can effectively cross over ghosts, this is the time to do it. I recommend that everyone participate in the crossing in an unintrusive way. All the team members should sit silently and build their energy in meditation. The person doing the crossing may need to access the collective energy from the group to do the crossing. There should be *no* talking or shuffling around. Be respectful! Allow the crossing to take place, and heal the location of residual energies. Tell the family or client that if they have any EVPs, they should not listen to them in the home after this point.

HAUNTED RECORDING

A client was hearing a dark entity speak through her husband's snores at night, so she recorded them. She brought the recording for me to listen to. I heard a threatening, deep voice say "F**k you" and "I hate you," just as she had explained. With her husband's permission, I did a healing on him and sent the dark entity away. When it was done, her husband felt peaceful and very calm. He mentioned that even the house seemed brighter.

Relieved, my client went out into the lobby and began to play the tape recording to her girlfriends. Everyone had chills because the voice sounded so sinister. For a moment, they all got caught up in the drama and played the recording over and over. I warned her that she would need to destroy the tape and advised her not to play it anymore. She immediately grabbed the cassette out of the recorder—but it was too late. The tape recorder began to turn itself on and off on its own. The energy of the entity had reattached almost as if it had been called through playback. We had to do a healing on the tape recorder and sent the entity away again.

Energy is real. As a paranormal investigator, you may have to educate your clients about how to keep their homes clear of unwanted energy. At the end of the investigation, it is okay to share the events of the night with the clients with discretion. Tell them that you will review the evidence and let them know if you captured anything else. This gives you a nice way to reestablish contact with the clients to find out if the location has settled down. It is very common to have increased activity after a typical investigation. However, if you are crossing over ghosts and clearing the home, the environment should be calm. If the homeowners have become attached to the excitement surrounding the haunting and the anticipated ghostly pranks, it may take their cooperation to eliminate the ghosts for good. They will need to stop feeding energy to the haunting and may need to learn how to cross over ghosts they encounter. Like I mentioned earlier, people drag stuff home with them all the time. If the paranormal team cleanses the home and it gets reinfested with supernatural activity, it is most likely new entities altogether. The homeowners must take responsibility for what they allow in their home and should learn to clear off their energy.

Of course, you will also have clients who want to verify a haunting because it can be good for business. In those cases, you will just seek to collect evidence of the haunting. While this could be seen as an ethical choice, just understand that if you disagree with it, you can pass it on to another group. Don't worry about judging the situation one way or another; just be clear about what type of work you want to do while investigating and stay true to that.

Many people love to visit haunted locations. There are haunted castles, haunted bed and breakfasts, and haunted battlefields all over the world that attract a healthy number of visitors each year. I enjoy traveling to haunted locations worldwide, and I would hate to take that away from other people because I imposed my own beliefs on it. So, just remember, do what you can for your clients and honor their wishes. Haunted locations also serve humanity because they continue to teach us and future generations about life after death and even a little history!

Okay, your team is packed up and you are ready to go .... I recommend a closing circle at this time. This gives each investigator a chance to examine the group to make sure that everyone is cleared of any attachments. Sometimes you may notice a team member getting really negative during an investigation. If this occurs, stop what you are doing immediately and do a healing on this team member or walk them out of the property. You may want to carry holy water in your equipment bag for situations like this. While they are rare, they do happen. Stay with your team member until they are back to themselves before you return to the investigation. Having a closing circle or closing prayer gives you one last chance to check out your team and make sure that they are clear to leave. We always thank the spirit world for allowing us to work with them for the benefit of proving that life after death exists. We tell them (if we don't cross them) that they are not allowed to come home with us.

If you forget to do this closing circle, you may notice that team members get flat tires on their way home, become so drowsy that they fall asleep behind the wheel, get into car accidents, or go home and fight with their families. Some team members will actually bring the haunting into their own home, which can wreak havoc on their family, health, and finances. The closing circle is a vital step in conducting a paranormal investigation.

We do this work to learn. We do this work to explore the unknown. Paranormal investigating is an adventure. But let's remember that the ghosts we hunt may be us one day. Let's always show respect for them in the field and help as many as we can to find their way home.

12: bizarre ghostly encounters

Working with the spirit world has been an awesome journey that has enhanced my life experience in many ways. There is no limit to the things ghosts and spirits can teach us. I have compiled many of my own personal experiences to share with you here. Sometimes it is easier to learn about ghosts and spirits through stories and real-life experiences. Reading this chapter will help to solidify your knowledge and ability to discern invisible influences that surround you. Keep an open mind, as all of these strange and bizarre encounters are true.

Haunted Cemetery

When I was growing up, my family lived near a section of woods that was inhabited by residents of a poor farm in the 1800s. Those woods had trails that we used for horseback riding, and we learned every hill and turn as we anticipated familiar low-hanging branches. My horse loved everything about those woods with the exception of one small hill near the heart of the trails. The hill was at a cross section where all the trails ventured off in different directions. The trail leading up the hill from that area was almost impossible to get my horse to climb. She would sidestep and rear to indicate that she wanted to remain at the bottom of the trail. With further insistence, she would gradually climb the slope with her head swaying back and forth wildly, the visible whites around her eyes showing to indicate something that startled her. We always referred to this horse as being "high-spirited" because she was very sensitive to her surroundings. Eventually, her behavior made more sense when we discovered a hidden cemetery at the top of that hill.

Covered beneath a century of overgrowth were three limestone headstones that were not visible from the trail. The discovery marked the beginning of my fascination with the potter's field, and I spent countless hours trying to name those left behind. It was about twenty years later that a historian from town determined that there were actually more than seventy bodies buried there in unmarked graves atop the hill. As a grown woman, I have revisited the site and have collected EVPs, orbs, and many intuitive impressions only to discover what my horse knew all along. That cemetery was haunted and she could see the ghosts at the top of the hill.

Ghosts That Choke the Living

I was choked by a ghost when I lived in a haunted house years ago. It happened during the peak of activity right after a paranormal group had come to validate the haunting in my home. I was sleeping in bed beside my future husband and awoke to the feeling of not being able to breathe. It literally felt like something heavy was sitting on my chest, with ghostly phalanges wrapped around my throat. I threw off the covers and sat up in bed heaving to get back my breath and then ran to the bathroom to splash cold water on my face. When I returned to bed, finally able to speak, I told my fiancé what had happened. At that point, he was still pretty new to the topic of ghosts and gave a halfhearted sympathetic response to reassure me. I had never been choked, nor had I ever felt unsafe amidst the ghostly activity that surrounded us before.

My fiancé had doubts about what I had told him until two weeks later when it happened to him! We were sound asleep when suddenly he awoke to being choked by a ghost. He was wide awake and experienced a sort of paralysis while not being able to move his arm to nudge me. He could not breathe and felt pressure on his chest. He tried to move his fingers and hands without success until finally, the entity moved away and he was able to sit up with force. This, of course, woke me up as he continued to gasp for air. Two weeks later, we moved.

My daughter and I had lived alone in the home for several years before meeting my fiancé. We had seen and experienced many things in our haunted house, including full-body apparitions of ghosts, EVPs, things being moved, cold spots, ghostly touches, and unexplained knocking and giggling coming from outside the second-story windows. It always felt like the ghosts looked after me and my daughter because we were the only ones who paid attention to them. We enjoyed the frequent yet odd interactions that we experienced from day to day. The ghostly activity seemed to peak each time I began dating someone new, and sometimes the ghosts flat out tried to chase men away. I always laughed about the responses guests would have and viewed it as some kind of test. May the best man win, I thought.

Through research, I discovered that the house had been built on top of an old cemetery and that the bodies had never been moved. In addition to the land being haunted, the home had seen its fair share of death as well. It was even owned by the local church at one point, and the parlor was said to have been used to view the dead.

As time went on, it seemed that more and more ghosts were coming to visit. We always referred to the resident ghosts as the ones who belonged there because they had lived in the house and died in it. They were wonderful, and we enjoyed sharing our home with them. However, once the others made themselves known, the house became overcrowded and the energy shifted dramatically. It no longer felt like a home that we would be safe in. At the time, I didn't know a very effective technique for crossing over ghosts, but through prayer we attempted to help as many as we could before we moved.

Our neighbors who lived in the other portion of the triplex experienced apparitions and frequent night terrors. A cable repairman experienced the feeling of being pushed down the stairs, on which I had seen frequent ghostly apparitions. Living in this home taught me many things about the spirit world, and I still feel grateful to the ghosts who resided with us there.

Lady with the Pearl Necklace

One evening, some friends and I gathered to use the scrying technique that I described in chapter 9. Two of our friends were scrying into each other's eyes from across a small table while my husband and I took photos of them with a digital camera. The results of the pictures were very interesting because the increased energy caused the photos to go slightly out of focus at times. It appeared that we were able to capture some of their past-life faces protruding outward from their physical faces. We also noticed that there was an entirely different image superimposed upon one of the sitters.

The image appeared to be the face of a young female spirit. She was looking straight into the camera with a big smile on her face. We could see that her hair was dark and that she wore it up in a bun or beehive hairdo, and it appeared that she was wearing a pearl necklace. The woman's face was not superimposed on top of our friend's face (which is often how you will see a past-life face), but rather it was slightly above her head. The photo was taken at a profile angle of our friend, and the ghost face was looking straight into the camera. It was an amazing capture, and we realized through further practice that this phenomenon occurs quite often.

The two people scrying increase their energy through a combined, concentrated effort. Ghosts and spirits are seen at a higher vibration than our own, so it makes sense that we would be able to tap into the spirit world by using this technique. Over the years, we have collected many photos of spirit faces captured while scrying.

Disembodied Arm

When we were young, my brothers and sisters and I told each other scary stories about disembodied ghosts that haunt the living. The purple fingernail doll was one of my favorite and scariest ghost stories. It was about a doll with purple fingernails that came alive at night and killed the family. Each morning, when another family member was found dead, the doll would have a bigger smile. When the little girl discovered that her purple fingernail doll was evil, she pulled off the arms and legs and put the dismembered doll in the trash can. But the following morning, the doll had put itself back together and came to get her. The story gave me nightmares, and I never forgot the image of the disembodied doll!

One night, I was invited to be a guest on a paranormal broadcast and brought a friend along for moral support. While we were filming the show, she hung out backstage and talked to the crew. My friend is also intuitive, so she and I have had many unexplained things happen when we are together.

After the show, we drove back to her place for a sleepover. I got nestled in on the sofa and began to fall asleep when I began to hear knocking on the wall. My friend's house was surrounded by a tall concrete wall, so I knew that the knocking was not from a living person. I was too tired to get up and deal with it, so I decided to ignore it and take care of it in the morning. The knocking continued and I threw the covers over my face to resume sleep, wishing it would just leave me alone!

My friend was in the adjoining bedroom with the door closed, so she was unaware of all the knocking and the ghost trying to get my attention. But suddenly, something woke her up. She sat straight up in bed and saw a disembodied arm in the corner of her room. The arm was bent and the hand was gesturing to say, "F**k you." She was shocked! Not only did she have a disembodied arm in her bedroom, but it was flipping her off! Just as the reality of what was happening began to sink in, the arm started to move closer to her very quickly. It flew across the room and ended with the middle finger right up in her face. At that point, she covered her face and began to pray the Archangel Michael prayer (see chapter 13).

In the morning, I told her about the knocking I had heard and then she recounted her evening with the disembodied arm. I couldn't believe she hadn't woken me up to tell me! Quickly, I went up to connect to the light and scanned the house intuitively. Her prayer had definitely worked, because the home was filled with light and there were no creepy energies hanging around. In retrospect, it seemed rather funny, because what else could a disembodied arm do to get someone's attention other than knock or give a hand gesture?

Lady with the Pointy Eyebrows

When my husband and I moved into our old Victorian home, he removed the vanity mirror in the guest bathroom and replaced it with a much fancier one. I then took down his new mirror and rehung the old round one. There was something special about that mirror, and even though it was aged with patina, it seemed magical.

My daughter was the first one to realize that the mirror was special. She was washing her hands one day as she gazed into the mirror at her reflection, but it was not her face looking back at her. Without telling me what had happened, she urged me to look into the mirror for a few minutes to see if I experienced anything unusual. She stepped outside the room, and I began to focus on my face in the mirror. It didn't take long before I noticed that my face was changing and that entirely different people were appearing where my face should be. The wallpaper behind me started to spin as if a vortex existed on the bathroom wall. When I emerged from the bathroom with a shocked look on my face, we shared what we had both experienced. Mirrors have often been used as instruments for seeing into the spirit world and are sometimes thought to be portals to other dimensions. The one face we had both seen was a woman with light-colored hair and dark, filled-in, pointy eyebrows.

My sister came for a visit, and we told her to look into the mirror and share anything that she saw. She came out right away and told us about the lady with the pointy eyebrows. We were amazed that she could see her, too. We didn't know anything about this woman and didn't know where she had come from.

That night, my sister had a dream that explained who the woman with the pointy eyebrows was and how she had arrived at our house. Apparently, she was attached to something that we had purchased and she needed our help. I have always made it a habit of clearing the energy off used items we bring into our home, no matter if they come from an antique store, auction, or friend. But I had let a few things slip past me because my husband had purchased them as a surprise. As I tried to recall any items that might be responsible for the ghostly attachment, it came to me. My husband had purchased an heirloom picture of the Last Supper from an older gentleman who had inherited it from his grandfather. The story fit in with the impression my sister had gotten in her dream, so I connected to the light and intuitively scanned the picture for an attachment. Sure enough, there she was—the lady with the pointy eyebrows!

I crossed the lady with the pointy eyebrows into the light, and we have never seen her face in the mirror again.

London Blob

That's right, London Blob, not London Fog! In 2010 I traveled to England to attend classes at Arthur Findlay College, which is billed as the "world's foremost college for the advancement of spiritualism and psychic sciences." The college sits just outside of London in a town called Stansted. People travel from all over the world to attend classes there and learn from some of the finest mediums and teachers.

When you attend classes, you study from 9:00 AM to 9:00 PM, eat all your meals on campus, and sleep in dorm rooms.

I shared a room with two other women and ditched an afternoon seminar to take advantage of my empty room so that I could nap. After about an hour, something startled me and I opened my eyes. Way across the room, my eyes focused in on something that was hovering over my roommate's bed. The dark gray blob was about two and a half feet long and looked like a jelly-filled sack of dark gray liquid with black dots. It vibrated as it moved slowly across the ceiling as if it were crawling.

I blinked my eyes a few times and sat straight up in bed. It was still there. I watched it wiggle from the corner across the entire width of the ceiling and then start down the wall. All I could think of was that it was headed my way and I needed to get rid of it. So I raised my hand as if I were some kind of wizard and cast light from my hand to the blob with a powerful prayer. In an instant, it disappeared. My heart was racing. "Why did I do that hand thing?" I asked myself. "What a dork! What was that?!" My heart was still racing and I jumped to my feet just as one of my roommates walked in.

I asked her if she had seen or felt anything strange while sleeping over there, and she replied that she had not. Then I told her what I had seen. She said that she didn't believe in any dark energies or dark spirits of any kind and then remarked that she would not be able to let spirits use her body when she slept if she believed in such things. Here's me: "WTF?! You do what?!" She then went on to explain that she tape-records herself while she sleeps at night and tells the spirit world that whoever wants to talk through her can use her body while she is sleeping. I tried to understand where she was coming from, but her viewpoint didn't make sense to me.

I explained to her that if a person had been evil while they were living, they would be evil after death until they went to God to be healed. With our free will, we can turn away from God while we are living and after death. I told her that using her body was like accepting a blind date online with anyone, and not believing that bad people (or ghosts) existed could be very dangerous. Then she told me that Spiritualists don't believe in ghosts that need to be crossed over and that there is no such thing as evil or dark energy. We had to agree to disagree because we had radically different views.

The following day, the roommate who slept beside the bed with the blob fell ill. She had a terrible migraine and felt too nauseous to attend classes. She stayed in bed for a day and a half before she emerged. I wondered what the gray blob was and if it had made my roommate sick. When it appeared to me, it was directly over the two beds in the far corner. Was it something that they had brought with them from home? Was it something that my roommate had attracted while asleep? Or was it something that had appeared because the building itself was haunted?

It is said that Arthur Findlay College sits upon land that has known origins dating back two thousand years. The grounds were reportedly built over Roman ruins, which they hope to excavate someday. The castle-like Stansted Hall has a fascinating and long history itself. The structure was burned down and rebuilt several times and was loaned to the Ministry of Defense to be used as a convalescent hospital for soldiers during World War II. Going to Arthur Findlay College was like attending a grown-up, real-life Hogwarts. Although I didn't see the blob again, I knew that I was safe. I had set up boundaries around my bed and filled the area around me with light.

Ironically, the following year, the college added a class for paranormal investigators to include the topic of ghosts. Good move, Arthur Findlay College! Paranormal investigating is now accepted as a method of mediumship.

Lion Figurine

Our paranormal investigation team was on location at a well-known haunted site when we experienced something being thrown. It was late into the evening and everyone had decided to pack up and call it a night. The team scurried around to take down the tripods and cameras while others attempted one last EVP session. When they captured the voice of a playful child, they called the rest of the group in to hear the recording. It was silent as we all strained to hear the ghostly child voice. Just then, something in the adjoining room made a thud as it hit the floor. The room was completely empty, as all the investigators were still crowded around the table together. We quickly turned our focus to the room where the noise had come from and saw a lion figurine lying in the middle of the room on the wood floor. The figurine had been sitting with several others on an end table along the far wall. Sometimes ghosts will become most active when the cameras are being packed up at the end of an investigation. It's like they don't want us to leave, and that's usually how our investigations get extended through the night!

Cavalry Ghost

While investigating the paranormal, we encountered a ghost that fought in the Civil War. All communication was recorded as EVP answers to our questions. This was one of the most remarkable conversations I have ever witnessed between the spirit world and the living. We asked what role the soldier had played, and he said, "Artillery." We asked how long he had been in the war, and he responded, "In it for too long. Can any of you help me?" When asked if he had been injured, he said, "Oh my god, it hurts here." We asked how much he had been paid, and he replied, "Just a little over 356 dollars." I thought the figure seemed too high for the Civil War era, so after the investigation, I did some research. The average white soldier made between thirteen and sixteen dollars per month, and the Civil War lasted approximately four years. So even on the low end of thirteen dollars per month, if this soldier served for just over two years, the dollar figure would be correct. I was amazed at the connection we established with that ghost but was saddened by the fact that he was still in pain.

Settlers Buried in Mound

A group of us headed out to investigate a large Native American burial mound. Rumors suggested that there were some settlers who were buried within the mound. We wanted to try out our Spirit Box and began asking questions to see if we could validate the rumor. We asked, "How many settlers were buried here?" Immediately, a voice responded through the box and said, "Three." We looked at each other with excitement and thought it was incredible to hear feedback right away. Then we asked the question again, just to be sure. "How many settlers were buried here?" A moment later we heard, "Three," loud and clear. One of our team members who thought he was being clever decided to ask again. Perhaps he wanted to test the accuracy of the device or the ghost that we apparently were talking to. So he asked the same question again. "How many settlers were buried here?" For the third consecutive time, we heard the answer, "Three." It was the same voice all three times and a little louder with each answer. Although it is not necessary to tape-record a Spirit Box session, it does confirm the evidence upon playback. We tape-recorded this session, and it served as a great piece of paranormal evidence.

Visits from Loved Ones in Spirit
Lilac Trees

My fiancé was traveling through the mountains of Georgia on his way to marry me. We had planned a beach wedding on the island of Captiva with a few close friends. As he was driving along, he thought of all the loved ones that we had lost and that we wanted to attend our special day. Just then, he drove past a row of lilac trees with an unseasonal bloom. He remembered that lilacs were my grandma's favorite flower and considered it a sign from her. He grabbed his camera and took a picture of them to surprise me with.

When he arrived in Florida, he told me about the strange lilac trees and mentioned that he only saw them on that one stretch of highway. He felt sure that the lilacs were a sign from my grandma and couldn't wait to show me the picture. We loaded the smart disc onto the computer and were disappointed when all that showed up was a blur. I decided to save the picture in my "unexplainable" folder and went to cook dinner.

Nearly six months later, we were surfing through old files on the computer when I decided to revisit the "unexplainable" folder. I selected the photo and double-clicked the icon, and it opened up full screen on my monitor. My husband and I literally screamed when we saw the image of my little sister who had passed! There was no question that it was her! My grandma has been known for bringing through my sister from the spirit world, so it confirmed to us that they both were with us on our special day.

Morphing Spirit

There is a phenomenon that suggests that a grieving person will think they see their loved one after they pass. I have experienced this happening and can vouch for the authenticity of it. This is actually known to happen when our deceased loved one is trying to let us know that they are still around.

Two weeks after my best friend died, my husband and I had a house-warming party. Many of our guests were mutual friends with the deceased, so there was a mixture of laughter and tears. We felt bad that our friend had died before he could see our new house, but that evening he came to see it from the spirit world!

We took random pictures throughout the night and, after the party was over, reviewed them. Of course, there were orbs and some strange light anomalies, but what captured our attention was the white glowing image in the kitchen window. There was no deck under the second-story window, nor was there any outside light. We loaded the picture onto the computer so we could see the image better and almost dropped to our knees. The image in the window appeared to be our friend who had just passed. He looked younger than he had when he died, but we knew it was him. There he was, peeking in our kitchen window to let us know that he had made it to our party!

Later in the year, a group of us were gathered at a local bar that had been a regular hangout for our friend who had passed. We were in mid-conversation when a stranger caught the attention of several of us at the same exact time. All our words just hung in the air as our gaze became transfixed on the man in the crowd. He appeared to all of us to be our departed friend. We watched as he turned and walked away, with the same swagger in his step. His forearm was freckled the same way, and his hair was an exact match—not an easy task, because our friend was quite exact when it came to how he wore his hair. We all stood there breathless and speechless. The man took a few more steps and then morphed back into his own normal form. At this time, we all looked at each other to make sure that we were not the only ones who had witnessed the transformation. The apparent hopeful shock on everyone's faces suggested that we all had seen the same thing.

It is my belief that when a spirit wants to be seen, they can use a living person's light to illuminate their image. The living person seems to morph into the deceased for just a moment and then returns to their original form. I have seen this phenomenon many times since then and know that it is a real experience! If you have lost a loved one and people tell you that you are crazy because you think you see them everywhere, know that you are *not* crazy! This is indeed spirit contact. Your loved one is doing whatever they can to appear to you so that you will know they have not left you and never will.

Lady of the House

A contractor was working on the second-floor hallway of our home when he put down his tools and came running outside to find me. He asked if I could come and stand by him while he worked for a while. Of course, I was startled by his request and asked him why. Then he began to tell me about the ghost of the old woman he saw standing on the landing of the stairs, watching him work. He described her in such detail that I knew he had seen her. I had seen her intuitively but had not experienced her with my eyes, yet she was a big reason why we had purchased the house.

My husband had found an old Victorian home listed for sale, and it was our dream to one day own one. I was hesitant to view the house because it was farther away from our hometown than I wanted to live. The next day, I scheduled a raindrop therapy massage, and the practitioner told me to focus on one thing during our session that I wanted clarity about. The only thing that came to mind was where we should move. During the session, I relaxed into the table and allowed the oils and massage to open my mind. I saw the image of a blue house with white trim followed by tremendous light.

When my session was finished, I retrieved the picture my husband had given me only to discover that it had the same roof lines as the house in my vision. But the house was not blue with white trim, it was light green. I wondered if it could be the same house and decided that I would need to see the house in person. My daughter and I drove to the property and peeked in the windows of the vacant Victorian home. Indeed, the roof lines matched. The home was so beautiful and seemed structurally sound.

That evening, the lady of the house came to me in a dream. Her energy was gracious and welcoming as she gave me a tour of the home. She was proud to show me the original fireplace and pointed out the quality craftsmanship that had gone into it. When I awoke, I knew that we were going to love the inside of the house as much as we already loved the exterior. It seemed that the lady of the house wanted us to live there because we were a good fit for it and the house was a good fit for us.

We toured the home in the morning and immediately knew that it was our destiny to own it. My daughter and I waited in the basement with my father-in-law until my husband could join us. We wanted to see the house together for the first time. A moment passed and I heard heavy work boots walk across the wood floor above us. I immediately thought my father-in-law had sneaked upstairs without us, but just then he came around the corner from another basement room. Yes, this house had spirits.

When my husband joined us, we toured the house together. On the third level, my daughter said that someone was touching her and lifting the back of her hair. The spirits were showing themselves to us in different ways, and they wanted us there. The interior was just as the lady had showed me in my dream, and the house was exactly what we had prayed for.

We made an offer on the house that very same day, and I continued to do research on the property. I discovered that the house had been run as a bed and breakfast several years earlier, and when it was in operation, it had been painted blue with white trim. The photos were still accessible on a tourist website—confirmation of my vision. Our dream was to own a bed and breakfast, which made it more interesting that my vision of the house appeared to match what it had looked like when it had actually operated as a B&B. There was no doubt that we had been led to our home and that our dream had actually reached out and grabbed us.

I also discovered articles that were written about the original owners of the property that all supported the qualities I had encountered in the lady of the house. She was said to have been a gracious host and had been known for her hospitality and kindness. The article said that she had been very beloved and had been thought of fondly by everyone in town. Her obituary mentioned that she had died in a covered carriage on her way home and had been placed in the parlor of the house until the funeral. She and her husband had owned and operated the hotel in town and had raised seven children. Three generations of their family had lived in the home as recently as the 1970s.

We often have strange occurrences at the house and have come to call our visitor "the lady of the house." She seems especially fond of the bedroom at the end of the hall and opens the door to the room all the time. I have awakened in the middle of the night to hear her humming a sweet tune as she walks past our bedroom door on the second floor. She does not have the dense or weakened energy of a ghost but rather seems to be visiting the house and new family out of love. We are always thrilled with a visit from the lady of the house and enjoy her presence when she comes.

Cigars and Cologne

The moment we purchased our Victorian home, my husband and I wanted to find pictures of the original family to hang on our walls. We were able to find some photos at the historical society and tracked down some living ancestors of the family. At Christmas time, the great-great-grandchildren of the original owners came to see the house, meet us, and hand-deliver some family photos. It was fun to show them around the house and share stories about the history of the property. Before they left, they all signed our guestbook in the dining room.

My husband and I walked them out when they left, and when we returned to the house, we smelled cigar smoke. The smell seemed to be central to one area in the home—and just hovered around our guestbook. Prior to the family members' visit, there was no smell and none of the family smoked. However, in one of our favorite pictures of their great-great-grandfather (the original owner of this house), he is posed in his finest clothes with a big cigar in his mouth.

Since that time, we have noticed the frequent smell of cigar smoke and sometimes the smell of cologne. Both smells originate in the area around our guestbook, and many people have detected walking through the area and smelling something. Perhaps he returns to his home from time to time just to check on things.

Hi, Girls

One afternoon I was staging an estate home with my assistant. The father had just passed away, and the daughter hired me to help her make the home market-ready. On the third trip out to my truck to retrieve totes filled with props, I noticed a shiny quarter. I hadn't noticed it before, so it struck me as odd. I picked it up and looked at the date: 1951. It didn't carry any significance for me, but I put it in my pocket just in case. I had gotten used to strange things happening and noticed that they sometimes made more sense later.

As the day wore on, my assistant and I were moving furniture from the lower level of the home up to the main floor. We were about halfway up the stairs when we heard an audible male voice say, "Hi, girls!" We knew that we were the only living people in the house, and we looked at each other with our eyes and mouths wide open. We had both heard the same thing!

We realized that the father was probably still in the home watching over things and were happy that he was friendly. Although we were alarmed, we continued to work. As the props ran short, we began to sort through the closets for additional decorations to use. My assistant found a quarter collection and brought it to my attention. I hadn't told her about the quarter that I had found and wondered if it could be a sign from the father.

After the job was complete, my client sent me a thank-you note with her e-mail address on it. Suddenly, it all made perfect sense. Her e-mail address was her first name, underscore, last name, and then the numbers 1951 (the year she was born), and the quarter I found was from 1951! That was confirmation to me that the quarter was meant for my client and that her father was trying to let her know that he was still around.

I sent the quarter to my client with an explanation of events that I was happy to finally understand. It was so beautiful that her father had tried so hard to reach her to acknowledge how hard she was working on his estate. She was very dedicated and had taken on more than any other family member, so the message served as a gesture of appreciation from her father in spirit.

Glowing Lungs

One of my clients came to see me for a healing session that began, as usual, with an intuitive body scan. Immediately, I noticed glowing lungs hovering beside her. The lungs did not appear inside her body where they should have been if they belonged to her, so I knew someone else was present. Sometimes when that type of thing happens, I put it aside and know that it will make more sense later. About halfway through our session, my client began to open up about some unhealed grief she had regarding the loss of her father. Immediately, it was apparent who the lungs belonged to. I asked her if her father had had lung problems and discovered that he had died of emphysema and could not breathe. Her father came in spirit to help his daughter heal and appeared to me in a way in which we could quickly identify him. Upon my client telling me her father's name, I was able to connect directly with him to validate his presence. This was an especially powerful session, and I was very grateful to be shown how much her father still loved her and wanted to help her heal.

Firefighter Father

I was doing a Theta Healing demonstration when I became aware that the man I was working with had a loved one present. As I was working on his shoulder pain, I intuitively saw large flames. When I asked him if his shoulder injury was somehow related to fire, he said that he used to be a firefighter. He was not able to work because of his injury. I redirected my focus and realized that there was a spirit with him. It felt like a father energy, so I inquired if this person's father had passed. Not only had his father passed, but he had also been a firefighter and had injured his shoulder— the same shoulder that my client was having pain in. It became clear that my client was a sensitive and was absorbing his father's pain without knowing it.

Oftentimes when our loved ones in spirit come close to us, we can identify them by feelings or smells. However, we don't want to take on their pain and sometimes need to ask the spirit to back away a bit. I have encountered people who have literally absorbed a deceased loved one's illness as a way of staying connected to them. It was clear how much my client loved and missed his father. We did some healing around his father and my client to release the need for him to carry the shoulder pain for his dad. The following day, the client told me that he could raise his arm above his head without pain and that it was healed. He hadn't had that range of motion for years and was thrilled with the outcome!

A Mother's Smile

While doing a Theta Healing session with a client one day, I literally saw her mother's spirit. My client had lost her mother a few months earlier and wanted help healing her grief. We were about a half hour into our session when we began to hit on some mother issues that still needed to be healed. When I'm in session with someone, I spend half the time with my eyes closed. I will ask my client questions while looking into their eyes, and then I will close my eyes while I am doing the healing portion of the session. I had just finished clearing some beliefs for my client and opened my eyes to focus on her again. When I opened my eyes, I saw her mother's spirit looking back at me. I blinked to clear my vision, but she remained. Her face was superimposed right on top of my client's face, just a foot or two away from my own. Of course, I knew who it was immediately. A minute passed and her mother was still there, just smiling back at me.

At this time, my client asked if her mother was present. She said that she could feel her mother's energy all around her and that her entire body was tingling. I was so relieved that I was able to tell her yes. Her mother had attended the session that day to receive part of the healing. Her presence served as a powerful confirmation of how the spirit world works. Her mother had passed, but she was still very present and active in her daughter's life. We both received a gift that day. My client got to feel her mother's presence and know beyond a shadow of a doubt that she was still with her, and I got to see her spirit with my eyes wide open.

Demons

Jump-in Demon

Years ago, I experienced a demon that jumped into my sleeping body and almost caused a heart attack. My husband was out of town and we were living in a new home, in a new state. I had my daughter sleep in my room so I could make sure she was safe. Her room was way across the house and I didn't know too much about our neighborhood yet. We both fell asleep as usual. Sometime in the middle of the night, I became aware that there was something or someone in our bedroom. The moment I detected the presence across the room, the shadowy figure jumped into my body. My heart immediately pounded against my chest and continued to beat harder than it ever had before. For a moment, I wondered if it would make me have a heart attack. I also wondered if this could be the reason other people died suddenly of heart attacks while they slept. Pound, pound! I sat straight up in bed with my hands to my heart. My daughter also sensed something and woke up. She sat straight up and exclaimed, "Mama, are you okay?!" I told her I was fine and that she should lie back down. As soon as she did, I mentally said very sternly, "Get the f**k out of my body! This is a vessel of light and you don't belong here!"

Just as suddenly as the entity had entered my body ... it left. My heart began to beat normally again. But I wanted to make sure that it was really gone and not just out of my body. What if it attacked my daughter next? After scanning the room with my eyes open, I closed my eyes and scanned the room intuitively. I connected to the Creator and made the command to send away any dark entities in or around our home and to fill our home with protective light. I also called in angels to watch over us while we slept. The entity was immediately gone, and we were safe.

Fire and Cinders

One time while in class, one student was doing a remote viewing on another student's home. She said she saw something red in her living room and thought she detected a red sofa. The next remote viewer saw something red and thought it must be red walls. Something seemed suspicious to me, and I decided to take a look for myself. What I saw was actually a big red demon in the middle of her living room. She shared her concerns about one of her family members who had been arguing with himself out loud and acting depressed and moody. It was clear that he had become the target of something dark.

I went up to connect to the light and made the command for the demon to go back into God's light. Intuitively, I saw the demon burst into flames immediately. That surprised me because usually they look like black energy that goes into the light. Sometimes they look like creatures or have an unusually large and scary face. This was the first time that I had seen one turn to fire, so I stayed with the vision and watched as it continued to burn for a few more seconds, and then the entire thing turned to cinders and went up into the light. The student said that when she returned home, there was a marked improvement in the way her home felt as well as the attitude of the family member she was concerned about.

Ape Man

On a plane leaving Las Vegas, I was nestled into my seat preparing to doze off when I intuitively saw a large ape-like demon run from the front of the plane and shove his face right up to mine. He cocked his head in a curious fashion as if to see who I was or if I could see him. I opened my eyes for a moment and looked around to see who had brought this beast onto the plane. What kind of havoc could he cause? I wondered. Did he have the strength to mess with the navigation devices in the cockpit? I didn't know, but I did know that I would not get the rest I wanted unless I got rid of the creature. I closed my eyes and connected with the Creator and made the command to send it back to God and to transform it back into light and love. It only took a second. Bleep. Gone. I scanned the rest of the plane, and it was clear, too. Then I fell asleep.

Bilocation Demon

A friend called to tell me about someone she knew who was being haunted by a demon. I led her through the clearing process, confident that she could get rid of it for her friend. A few minutes later, I received a second phone call from her sounding rattled. She had remotely cleared the demon from the property of her friend but instantaneously felt the creature standing right beside her. She heard insidious heavy breathing and groaning. I linked in quickly and intuitively witnessed a large red creature with glowing eyes that had jumped from one location to the next. I quickly made the command to send it back to God. Immediately, the creature was gone. My friend was relieved that it left so quickly and never returned. When we reviewed her process, she realized that she had forgotten to clear herself off after she had done the clearing. Dark entities will sometimes try to sneak down the light after you have cleared them, so you must slam the door shut behind them once they have gone up into the light—and then clear your own energy. Simply rub your palms together and then push the entity's energy away from you with one hand as you pull your energy back with the other hand (see the "Energy Break" section in chapter 13). You could also imagine that you are separating your energy with an invisible knife, or wave your hand over your body and head.

Portals and Multiple Entities

I received a call from a local paranormal group that had been working with an older woman who was haunted. She had lived in her house for many years and then suddenly started seeing things. She didn't mind seeing loved ones who had passed, but she was also experiencing some darker entities. She saw red eyes staring at her through her pictures on the wall and experienced things moving on their own.

Upon entering the home, one team member got a head-ache and knew something was out of whack in the environment. She called in another paranormal investigator who discovered that the house had extremely high EMF readings. High electromagnetic frequencies can contribute to paranormal occurrences because ghosts can use those high frequencies to charge themselves. The client had also been experiencing headaches, which can also be connected to the high EMFs. When the investigator used his tri-field meter, the needle moved rapidly to the highest mark. He was familiar with high EMF readings because he had experienced them in his own home. He was determined to remedy the situation and had devised an instrument that solved the problem. Brilliant! Now he helps other people lower the harmful EMFs in their own homes.

He made the alteration for the client, and it dramatically reduced the level of EMFs entering the property. The EMFs remained just slightly above normal but well within the safe range. The client's headaches went away almost immediately. The team made numerous visits and all were very beneficial, but when the woman began seeing creatures, they called me.

Many paranormal investigators are afraid to encounter dark entities. While it's true that they can attach to you and follow you home, the fear you have of them actually magnetizes them to you and gives them power.

The client was really scared when she began seeing a creature that looked half human and half monkey. I had experienced this type of creature before and knew that they responded very quickly to clearings. I knew the members of the group to be very dedicated investigators and wanted to show them how to clear a home of dark energy without being afraid. It has always been my experience that clearing a dark entity is just as easy as clearing a ghost or doing a healing.

We arrived at the client's house with a game plan. I did my walk-through to familiarize myself with the property and catch up with the others who had been there previously. Most of the investigators had experienced apparitions and unexplained things personally. After viewing the property, we all came together to discuss our findings. We were all in agreement that several portals were open and that they served as doorways for discarnate entities to enter through.

We held hands in a circle as I led the team up to connect in the theta brain wave. I made the command to see and know where the portals were that needed to be closed and that were not beneficial to the client or were potentially harmful. A moment later, the group members opened their eyes and said that they all saw the locations. We went back and connected to the light, and I commanded that all the portals be closed now. Almost instantaneously, the team opened their eyes and said that they all witnessed the portals closing throughout the house. Afterward, we walked through the house to verify that the odd feelings we had experienced earlier had been neutralized.

We lit some incense and a white candle and then formed another circle by holding hands. This time, I made the command for all lower-level energies, ghosts, and creatures to go into the light now. Whenever working with a group in this way, it is important that one person make the command. It doesn't matter who it is, but one person should take that role. We were connected to the light and witnessed many entities leaving. We then did a healing for the souls of the client's loved ones who had passed. We wanted to make sure that if they came back to visit, they would have moved into the light so that their presence would not be harmful to her. While the group was silent, I asked for the name of the one that needed to be called by name in order to leave. I was given the name, and commanded it to go by its name. It moved out quickly. When we were finished with the house, I did one final healing on the client herself. When I made the command to remove anything attached to her, I witnessed a dark silhouette leave and go into the light. I then brought down light and unconditional love from the Creator to heal her.

It was determined through talking with our client that she began seeing things after recovering from a surgery several years earlier. She just woke up and was able to see entities, she said. That is not at all unusual. Some people's clairvoyance is triggered by an injury, sudden life change, or surgery. I explained to the client that she would continue to see things because she was clairvoyant. She mentioned seeing spirits at the grocery store and her family's houses when she visited. It was our job to reassure her that it was okay and that she could get rid of anything that she didn't want in her home. We used the circle of light to create a one-way-only portal of light that would take anything back to the Creator. Just by connecting into the theta brain wave and commanding it, we moved the portal of light outside into the yard. We told the client that whenever she encounters anything that makes her feel uncomfortable, she can command it into that light and it will go away for good.

We pulled back the curtains and opened the windows to allow a physical shift to take place in the home, and it felt clear and harmonious when we were done.

It is my personal belief that more people will begin to experience spiritual beings of all kinds. We are just beginning to grasp the infinite number of spiritual dimensions and entities that exist. It is very important not to be fearful but to be armed with techniques that work. Perhaps opening (one-way-only) portals of light all over the world is what is needed to keep the balance.

13: protection

It is extremely important to protect yourself while working with ghosts and other supernatural beings. The way you protect yourself will depend on your own spiritual development. Some people tend to attract more discarnate entities to them than others. Such a person is often referred to as a "ghost magnet." This does not mean that anything is wrong with the person. It only means that they will need to clear off energetically and protect themselves more. When you get used to raising your vibration and feel confident crossing over ghosts, they will be less bothersome to you. Please don't get caught up in ego. It just is what it is, and only you will know if you have to be more vigilant than others. Honor where you are, and it will be easy to ascertain your level of spiritual development.

If you are new to working with the paranormal or you are an investigator who has gotten lazy, let's go over some protection techniques. First of all, when you are called into the home of someone you don't know, you have no idea what type of energy you will encounter. So be prepared. That means that you should always center yourself and clear your head before you even enter their space. You should be doing what you can to raise your personal vibration through prayer or meditation. It is a great idea to join hands with your fellow investigators to create a protective circle before you begin each investigation.

My favorite prayer for protection is well accepted among paranormal groups and is the "Prayer to Saint Michael the Archangel." It doesn't matter what religion you follow—the archangels are available for everyone. Archangel Michael comes right away when called, and if you are sensitive, you may see or feel his energy. This prayer can be ordered on a small holy prayer card (purchased online) and is very inexpensive. Or you can print out this prayer using your home computer. Each investigator in your group should have this prayer memorized or carry a copy of it with them in the field. It doesn't matter if you believe in heaven and hell the way religions teach them. This prayer is very powerful and works.

Prayer to Saint Michael the Archangel

Saint Michael the Archangel,
defend us in battle;
be our protection against the wickedness and snares of the devil.
May God rebuke him, we humbly pray:
and do thou, O Prince of the heavenly host,
by the power of God,
cast into hell Satan and all the evil spirits
who prowl about the world seeking the ruin of souls.
Amen.

Saint Benedict Medal

Another way to protect yourself is to wear something that has protective significance for you. For some, this could be the crucifix or the Miraculous Medal, although when someone is really being "attacked," I pull out all the stops and recommend the Saint Benedict Medal. It doesn't matter if a person is Catholic or not—the medal will still work. I recommend that this medal be blessed before it is worn. Traditionally, the medal was most powerful when it was blessed by a Benedictine priest. However, the Pope now allows any Catholic priest to bless these medals with the same protective attributes.

What makes this medal such a powerful amulet? The Saint Benedict Medal is inscribed with a powerful prayer and offers strong protection against demonic and negative spirits. On the back of the round medal, the cross is dominant. On the arms of the cross are the initials of a Latin prayer (CSSML NDSMD), which stands for *Crux sacra sit mihi lux! Nunquam draco sit mihi dux!* The translation in English is: *May the holy cross be my light! May the dragon never be my guide!* Above the cross is the Latin word *pax*, which means "peace"—it has been the Benedictine motto for centuries. Around the outside of the medal, there are more initials (VRSNSMV SMQLIVB), which represent the Latin prayer for exorcism: *Vade retro Satana! Nunquam suade mihi vana. Sunt mala quae libas. Ipse venena bibas!* This means: *Be gone, Satan! Never tempt me with your vanities. What you offer me is evil. Drink the poison yourself!*

Some of you will never encounter entities dark enough to use this with, and that is a good thing. However, some of you will be challenged by much darker forces, and it is important that you and your family and/or clients know how to overcome them.

Personal Amulet

A personal amulet is something that you make yourself to wear or carry for protection. This item can be anything from a basic rock to your grandma's wedding ring. It doesn't have to have significant meaning for you until you infuse it with the energy you desire. Let's say that you have something simple and common, like a nickel, that you wish to use for protection. Before the nickel has the power of protection, it will need to be blessed. It may be blessed by you or someone you know and trust. The nickel should be prayed over and used for meditation with the intention to hold protective properties. You should also make sure that it has the ability to ward off negative entities or any energy that could be potentially harmful.

Sometimes when I am creating a new protection amulet, I will dip it in holy water or allow the smoke of incense to surround it. If you choose to use incense, use one that has a high-vibrational scent and stay away from fruity, artificial fragrances. The best ones to use are frankincense and myrrh. I have also used Nag Champa (from India), which can usually be found at metaphysical bookstores or health food stores.

While you are holding your item of choice, concentrate on raising its vibration and sealing it with protective properties. You may ask your guardian angels or guides to help you. Once you have worked with an item in this way, it will hold the energy that you have infused it with. Even a common nickel will be able to protect you on an investigation!

Holy Water

Holy water is used as protection against negative energies as well as for cleansing a haunted location or person. Holy water can be ordered online, or you may be able to get some from your local parish or any church in town. I usually use holy water in combination with sea salt while doing cleansing rituals. You won't need to soak the place—just a light splash will do. You can dip your fingers in the holy water and, while saying your intention or prayer, fling the drips onto the walls, ceiling, and floor. It is helpful to light a pure white candle while doing this type of cleansing. As mentioned in chapter 4, holy water may also be used in the bathtub to soak in.

You may also make your own holy water to use for clearing and protection. As Dr. Masaru Emoto has shown us through his scientific study of water, it can be charged for whatever your intention is. In his book *The Secret Life of Water*, Dr. Emoto demonstrates how feelings and words can literally change the structure of water. If you wish to make your own holy water, just follow these simple instructions:

1. Fill a container with water and put the lid on it.

2. Write the word(s) on the container that you want the water to embody. This could be "Protection," "Healing," "Clearing," "Love," etc. It's up to you which words you choose.

3. Put the container in the freezer overnight. When the water freezes, the structure of the water crystals will change.

4. Take the frozen water out of the freezer and allow it to thaw naturally.

5. The water is ready to use.

You may also make your own holy water by filling a container with water and praying over it. Depending on the spiritual practices you follow, you may burn incense around the water or set powerful crystals or other amulets that you find to be beneficial by the water. You may meditate on the water and raise its frequency to hold clearing and protective properties. Sometimes it's best to charge the water every day for a week to increase its efficacy.

Sea Salt

Sea salt seems to repel dark energies and is often used as a means of protection. Once a person has cleared the space in their home, crossed over the ghosts, and made sure that there are no lingering dark energies, sea salt may be used to protect the space from recontamination. If you pour sea salt in front of your doors and put a pinch above your windows and doorways, it will work to seal your house from unwanted energies.

Soaking in sea salt is very cleansing and healing as well. If you ever feel like you have some dark energy following you around, take a long soak in a sea salt bath. Some people are just more prone to attachments and will need to cleanse themselves on a regular basis. Soaking in the ocean works the same way as a sea salt bath. Make sure to go underwater if you have an especially strong attachment.

Sage Clearing

Sage can be used to clear a home, person, land, vehicle, or item. This is especially useful for clearing residual energy. It will help you get rid of negative entities that were created by human emotions such as anger. It will not cross over a ghost or cast out a demon, but it will raise the vibration and help weaken the hold they have in their surroundings— which will make it easier to release them through other methods.

I prefer to use a white sage bundle that is dried and tied with string. When I burn the end of the sage bundle, I hold it over a bowl or seashell so the location is safe from falling ash or flame. Make sure that the smoke from the sage fills every corner of every room, including closets and cubby-holes.

As you are filling the corners with smoke, it works best to hold an intention or say a prayer. I prefer to say prayers out loud to fill the environment with the vibration of holy words. You can say any prayer you want, whether it be formal or made up. But make sure to call upon protection and light and allow any old, dark, negative, or low-vibrating energies to leave while allowing light-filled, peaceful, loving, and joyful energy to fill the home.

As soon as you have gone through the entire residence (garage included), it is important to open the windows and turn on all the lights to allow the home to air out. If there are any ceiling fans, turn those on for a few minutes to help clear out the smoke and transition the energy. You should notice a drastic change from when you started. Many years ago, I was clearing a house and actually saw black shadows moving and swirling on the walls trying to get away from me. I did not give in to my fear and continued with the clearing. When I was done, those energies were gone for good. After a home is cleared, it is up to the individual or family to keep it that way.

Crystals

Some people may be drawn to crystals or stones that offer protective properties, especially when dealing with negative energies. The following stones are known to raise your vibration.

Tektite

Tektite is well known for its ability to raise one's personal vibration and is used for protection against negative thoughtforms, spirits, and other entities.

Moldavite

Moldavite is a very high-vibrational stone and is my personal favorite. It is a form of tektite that is believed to be from a meteorite in the Czech Republic. It is known to help with quick personal transformation and offers protection to those in need. If this stone is right for you, hold it in your left hand and see if you can feel the vibration.

Black Obsidian

Black obsidian is known for its ability to cleanse the aura and provides powerful protective energies, assisting one in the release of negative patterns and the removal of negative energetic attachments.

Amethyst

Amethyst carries a high vibration that offers spiritual protection and purification.

Smoky Quartz

Smoky quartz is one of the premier grounding and anchoring stones and is strongly protective.

Black Tourmaline

Black tourmaline is a powerful stone for protection against negative energy of all kinds, as well as being a strong spiritual grounding stone. It is believed to be one of the best protection stones that you can use.

Herkimer Diamond

Herkimer diamonds are not usually associated with protection, but they are extremely powerful in raising one's personal vibration. They enhance the vision and clarity of your intuition and deflect negative energy from people who are weak-willed.

Years ago, a friend offered me a Herkimer diamond and told me to place it under my pillow while I slept. I had used many crystals over the years but had never experienced the type of effects that this tiny little stone created. All night long, I visualized flashes of light similar to fireworks going off in my head. I barely slept at all that first night, but over the next few weeks, my body adjusted to the extremely high vibration of the stone.

After a few weeks, I told my friend that my stone had quit working. For some reason, the light show had stopped and I could barely feel it pulsate in my palm. She gave a little giggle as she explained that my vibration had raised to match the stone's vibration. It wasn't broken in any way. It had worked well indeed. This is a wonderful stone to meditate with or use prior to an investigation.

Any of these stones can be carried in your pocket or worn around your neck. You may also sleep with one or several stones under your pillow. It is best to put them in a little satchel so they don't get tossed around during the night. Be sure to clear off your stones if you take them on an investigation with you so they can remain functional. Stones can get attachments, too—especially protective stones, which may actually absorb the negative energy in an attempt to keep you clear.

Energy Break

One way to clear your energy is by doing a simple energy break. This will disconnect your energy from anyone or anything that you have come into contact with. It can even be used to separate your energy from a person who seems to be draining you. Protection is done prior to and during spirit contact, and the energy break is what follows.

An energy break should be done to keep your energy your own. It will disallow anything to attach to you. Simply rub the palms of your hands together while holding them in front of you, with elbows bent. Then push your left hand outward in front of you to give back the unwanted energy as you pull your right hand inward to your body to collect your own energy.

You may use another technique that works for you as long as the intention is to create a break in energy. You could imagine that you are separating your energy with an invisible knife, or wave your hand over your body and head. If you find that you are thinking about another person's situation long after ending a conversation with them, you have absorbed some of their stuff. If you do the energy break, your mind should stop connecting to their issues.

Theta Healing

Theta Healing is used to protect people from negative energy attachments as well. In fact, if you do enough Theta

Healing on yourself, you won't need to use any physical means of protection. If you clear enough beliefs (some of which are literally from ancient times), your body will naturally hold a very high vibration and will become impervious to psychic attack and entity attachment. Once you have cleared beliefs and subconscious programs that make you a target for lower vibrations, you can reprogram yourself so that any lower vibration that attempts to attach to you is immediately sent into the light. In a way, you create a constant source of light around your physical body and won't need to address each entity one by one. As part of your progress through the spiritual levels, you will one day come to realize that you no longer need protection or to surround yourself in light ... because *you are the light.* We are all divinely connected to the light at all times unless we choose not to be through free will. Once we master the physical plane and understand how all these tools and techniques work, we can advance to being able to do it all without tools.

Honor where you are at. This is not a race. It would be harmful and irresponsible for you to rush out there unprotected without having advanced first through the different spiritual levels. Just know that you are on a journey and everything will get easier to master as you go.

conclusion

Some people are born open and are able to see spirits as children. Some retain that ability, while the majority lose it over time. Other people spontaneously open up when they hit middle age, survive a life-changing event, or have a near-death experience. Others may not experience the spirit world until their final moments of life. But one thing is for certain: the spirit world is all around us and is a natural part of life here on earth.

If you have not experienced the spirit world firsthand, the best place to start is with your own healing. Oftentimes we are so weighted down with limiting beliefs, fears, and judgments that we cannot access the higher-vibrational planes until we heal. I have known countless people who began a journey to heal their lives and ended up with psychic and mediumistic abilities. Those abilities were not actually what they were seeking when they began their journey, but were a natural outcome of the process.

When I embarked on my own journey of healing, I was favored with many abilities. I felt called to help people heal and knew that in order for me to do that, I needed to heal myself first. I needed to get rid of all my grudges, resentments, anger, and self-limiting thoughts. I had to dig into my subconscious mind to discover what emotions were poisoning me and what issues were holding me back. My life needed to be cleared of old baggage so that I would be able to access more light and healing energy. My quest for healing began when I was young, but the Theta Healing technique accelerated my progress dramatically. In addition to healing myself, I was finally able to access the spirit world at will. At last I was able to utilize my gifts and abilities to help people and fulfill my life's purpose.

I am able to use my abilities on paranormal investigations because I can detect ghosts and obtain information from them. Crossing over ghosts has become easy and nondramatic for me. When darker entities are detected, I can send them away too. I am able to communicate more effectively with the spirit world and can read the environment to obtain information about the history of a location.

Shamans, mystics, and Buddhist monks are able to access the theta brain wave through devoted prayer, fasting, and meditation. Most of us don't live in an isolated location or commit ourselves to living a life of prayer, and that is okay. We can still train our brains to use a slower brain wave to access the same state of awareness. Some people will be able to read this book and effectively reach the theta brain wave in an instant. They will be able to recite the commands and witness ghosts crossing over immediately. Some of you may feel like you would benefit from taking a class to learn from an experienced teacher. That's okay, too. Taking a class will teach you how to clear the fears and beliefs that limit you from reaching the theta brain wave at will. If you suspect that you may be blocking some of your own abilities, set up an appointment with a Theta Healer or someone else who knows how to clear limiting beliefs.

The law of attraction is a real, universal law, but it operates primarily with your subconscious mind rather than your conscious mind. Your subconscious mind is responsible for creating the life you are living today. Your conscious mind may know that you desire to live a different life, but it will not be able to get you there until your hidden subconscious beliefs are in unison. If you fear the unknown and are scared of something in the spirit world, it is almost guaranteed that you will draw that experience to you.

Fear is detected on the subconscious level and cannot be hidden from the spirit world. Just as animals can sense fear and know when to attack, entities do too. To ensure safety, be sure to use the protection and clearing techniques outlined in this book. You may also want to work on your beliefs to conquer any fears. Once you remove your fear programs, you will no longer draw dark entities or experiences to you and you will gain a deeper truth about the spirit world.

The information in this book will enable you to reconnect with those you have lost and will help you recognize the signs they send. You will be able to communicate with spirits and cross over ghosts. You will be able to send away dark entities without fear or struggle. Doing this work may help to reestablish your faith in an all-creative force that lives through us and all around us and cannot be destroyed. The more you heal and work with the techniques in this book, the more you will be able to see through the veil—until one day you will realize there is no veil at all. It is only your beliefs that separate the world of the living from that of the dead.

Always remember that God gave us authority over demonic spirits. It doesn't matter what belief system you adhere to; every human has this authority. When we command a demon spirit to go—while being connected to the light—then it must go. While quoting the Bible is not something I normally do, I feel this reading from Matthew 10:7–8 sums things up well:

> And as ye go, preach, saying, The kingdom of heaven is at hand.
>
> Heal the sick, cleanse the lepers, raise the dead, cast out devils: freely ye have received, freely give.

I interpret the words "raise the dead" to reflect our ability to help the dead by raising them into the light. Matthew was by no means talking about raising a zombie nation here on earth. To raise the dead means to find the lost souls and send them to God.

If you have been called to work with spirits and cross over ghosts, know that it is a divine calling. We are here to heal the sick and cast out devils. That means you ... and me ... and all of us. It is part of our divine inheritance, and we are supposed to know how to protect ourselves and keep our planet safe.

I encourage you to use this book to help you achieve your own connection with the spirit world, and I wish you joy and healing as you reconnect with loved ones on the other side.

To Write to the Author

If you wish to contact the author or would like more information about this book, please write to the author in care of Llewellyn Worldwide Ltd. and we will forward your request. Both the author and publisher appreciate hearing from you and learning of your enjoyment of this book and how it has helped you. Llewellyn Worldwide Ltd. cannot guarantee that every letter written to the author can be answered, but all will be forwarded. Please write to:

Diana Palm
℅ Llewellyn Worldwide
2143 Wooddale Drive
Woodbury, MN 55125-2989

Please enclose a self-addressed stamped envelope for reply, or $1.00 to cover costs. If outside the U.S.A., enclose an international postal reply coupon.